I0762742

TO

---

FROM

---

DATE

---

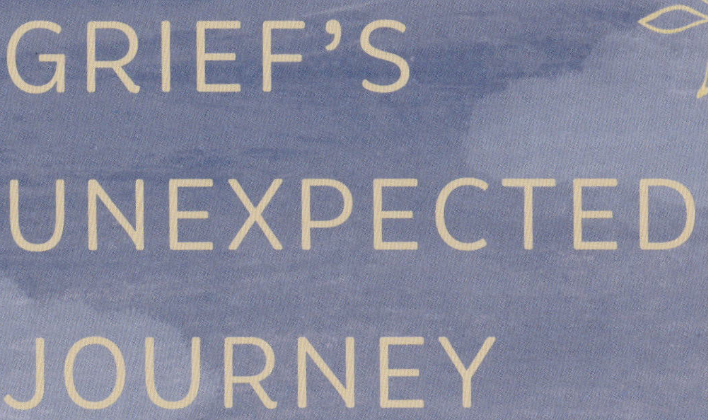

# GRIEF'S UNEXPECTED JOURNEY

*90 Comforting Devotions After Losing Someone You Love*

*Grief's Unexpected Journey: 90 Comforting Devotions After Losing Someone You Love*

First Edition, February 2025

Published by:

21154 Highway 16 East
Siloam Springs, AR 72761
dayspring.com



Written by: Paige DeRuyscher
Cover Design by: Jenna Wilusz

Printed in China
Prime: U2774
ISBN: 979-8-88602-875-1

# CONTENTS

# INTRODUCTION

I wrote this book after living through the darkest time in my life. It was something no one could have prepared me for, and something I never thought I would make it through. The journey of grief is indescribable to those who have not walked it. It is unique to each of us, but we do share one thing in common: a desperate need to know that God is with us through it all.

Within these pages, you'll find words of hope and encouragement; you won't find quick fixes or easy answers. I want to walk with you daily; to invite you into faith beyond feeling; to assure you of a love so great that it is covering every moment you experience and is working to heal your heart in ways you can't even imagine. You are precious to the One who made you, and you won't face one day without Him.

Each day of this devotional, I'll offer reminders of His presence, promises from His Word, and ways to take small steps of healing as you move through this season. Please hear these hopeful words from someone who has been there: there is no day too hopeless, no struggle too great, no darkness too deep that He can't carry you through. I hope you'll find that to be true as you walk this path of hope and healing with Him.

Paige DeRuyscher

# EVERY MOMENT MATTERS

*And we know that in all things*
*God works for the good of those who love Him,*
*who have been called according to His purpose.*
*ROMANS 8:28 NIV*

If you've ever gazed at a flickering candle long enough, you've likely noticed a change happening right beneath the flame. The once-hard wax begins to soften and turn to liquid, and if that candle is scented, its sweet aroma will start to fill the room. If candles had feelings, they would likely resist the match that lights them, preferring to stay unmelted, avoiding the burn, keeping their original, undisturbed shape.

When we experience the hardest times in our lives, it can burn in ways we never imagined. We most definitely would not have chosen to endure these seasons, and we may wonder how much more we can take before our loving God extinguishes the flame. First, we must remember that He never intended for us to feel the sadness of loss or the pain of brokenness. However, He does not allow a moment of our difficulties to be wasted. Whether we can see it now or will see it one day as we look back, He is orchestrating goodness within us, one day at a time. He is allowing us to become more like Jesus through it all. Like the wax of that burning candle, God softens our hearts in our grief. We learn what it is to bear the pain of a broken world, and we begin to recognize the deeper struggles in those around us. The more we open ourselves to His compassion, the more of that compassion pours through us to others. And not only are we softened, but we can offer the sweet aroma that only comes from those who have clung to Jesus through their darkest days. We, who have beheld His tender gaze, can offer His soul-soothing love to those who need it most. There's no rush, though—no matter where you are on the journey, just know every one of those difficult moments matters, and your loving Father assures you that not one will be wasted. May you feel His tenderness today.

***Lord, this life burns so much sometimes. I need to know You are bringing goodness out of the pain. May I sense the softening of my heart and find purpose in sharing Your love with others on the journey.***

# HIS VOICE

***"Be still, and know that I am God."***

***PSALM 46:10 NIV***

When we lose someone we love, we are often bombarded with overwhelming thoughts and feelings. We may be surrounded by others seeking to offer comfort and care for us through words and actions. And we may be confused by all that's happening around and within us; things may feel chaotic when we just want a sense of peace. Life can suddenly feel surreal, and it can sometimes be hard to sense God's presence, even though we know we need Him more than ever and we long for that sense of assurance He brings. When we're in the depths of our struggles, we just want to know, *How can I connect with You, God?* We know He is with us, but we need something more to hold on to.

In moments like these, it's good to remember that, as much as we are reaching out to Him, He is reaching out to us even more. It may take some time to identify, but as we listen with our hurting hearts, we can hear His still, small voice beneath everything we're experiencing. He is whispering words of hope and peace and comfort, assuring us that He is right here and will never leave our side. If we are able to pause amid everything we're going through, we can pray this simple prayer: *Lord, help me to hear You today.* Our thoughts and feelings can be loud and pressing, but the more we can pause and turn our hearts toward Him, even for a moment, the more attuned we will be to His voice.

We can also hear Him speaking Life to us through Scripture, any time of day: "'Though the mountains be shaken and the hills be removed, yet My unfailing love for you will not be shaken nor My covenant of peace be removed,' says the LORD, who has compassion on you" (Isaiah 54:10 NIV). Whether it's in the quiet of our hearts or in our reflections on His promises, He will speak. Be encouraged as you walk through what can feel like an overwhelming time. He is here, wanting you to know the comfort of His love and the assurance of His peace.

***Lord, help me to hear Your loving words in my heart.***

# THE ROAD AHEAD

*Jesus answered,*
*"I am the way and the truth and the life."*
*JOHN 14:6 NIV*

Why don't our hardest paths come with maps? Wouldn't it be wonderful if we could know exactly what was coming down the road so we could be prepared? Many people throughout history have surely cried out to God in this way: *Lord, I just need to see what's ahead. Please show me the way!* Grief, especially, can leave us feeling lost, even in the midst of our ordinary lives. Feelings may be unfamiliar; relationships may be strained; we may feel afraid to move forward in faith, wondering what might be lurking around the corner, waiting to steal our joy. We can feel frozen, struggling to trust God's leading and wishing life were more laid out for us. Most of us have been there at one time or another—called beyond the boundaries of our trust, wondering where the courage will come from for our next steps, maybe even crying out for God to make His presence known in a time that feels lonely and scary. In these times, it's good to remember that He has never left our side.

While our prayer for an easy-to-follow map may not be answered, the assurance that He is with us on the journey is there, even in the most confusing times. If you ever have trouble imagining Jesus's constant presence, try to envision Him in the light of the Gospels. Hear Him saying, "Let the little children come to Me" (Matthew 19:14 NIV) and see yourself as that child, cherished by Him, held safely in His arms. See Him washing His close companions' feet the night before He died for us, and count yourself among those companions. ". . .so He got up from the meal, took off His outer clothing, and wrapped a towel around His waist. After that, He poured water into a basin and began to wash His disciples' feet" (John 13:4–5 NIV). Remember that even those who walked with Him were uncertain about the road ahead, but they held on to that one promise—*I will be with you*—spoken and demonstrated in so many ways. That is our blessed assurance too. When you feel a little lost, you can count on your Navigator to bring you through. He is the Way, and you belong to Him.

***Lord, remind me of Your constant presence, and help me to rest in the moment with You.***

# TRUSTING HIS LOVE

***Trust in the Lord with all your heart and lean not on your own understanding; in all your ways submit to Him, and He will make your paths straight.***

***PROVERBS 3:5–6 NIV***

Let's talk about doubt for a moment. Any human being who has ever chosen to walk in faith has had to face the discouragement of doubt at one time or another. When life seems to be going well, we feel like we have all our ducks in a row. Maybe we've had a series of encouraging circumstances or a time of specifically answered prayers. When that happens, it can be easy to believe that God is *for* us—that He is our Healer, Deliverer, Redeemer, and Provider. After all, we have trusted Him, and He has shown up for us in so many ways. But when things take an unexpected turn, we can feel like the rug has been pulled out from beneath us. Those truths in Scripture that we have stood upon so confidently may now come into question; the voice of the enemy may whisper, "Are you *sure* you can trust Him?"

As we navigate the journey of loss, it is important that we cling to His promises, no matter what opposition we may face. It's during these difficult days that we learn to lean into God's goodness, even when we may be left with questions and disappointments that test our faith and threaten to move us away from Him. As His Word assures us, even in the darkest times, He isn't going anywhere: "The LORD Himself goes before you and will be with you; He will never leave you nor forsake you. Do not be afraid; do not be discouraged" (Deuteronomy 31:8 NIV). He is with us in our confusion and doubt, and He will provide encouragement as we press in.

If you find yourself struggling with something specific, reach out to a trusted mentor or friend who can point you in a positive direction. Don't allow fears to build up in your mind; speak up and find freedom from anything the enemy may be trying to use against you. God knew this would be part of your journey, and He has already provided all you need to make it through. Trust His heart of love for you, and you'll experience His promises in new ways, leading you to the brighter days ahead.

***Lord, protect my heart from doubt. Remind me of Your precious promises and help me to trust in You today.***

# THE WONDER OF CREATION

*In His hand are the depths of the earth, and the mountain peaks belong to Him. The sea is His, for He made it, and His hands formed the dry land.*

*PSALM 95:4–5 NIV*

Throughout the centuries, humans have pointed to nature as a mighty display of God's creative handiwork. "The heavens declare the glory of God," says Psalm 19:1, "the skies proclaim the work of His hands" (NIV). And throughout our lives, perhaps even before we believed in a Creator, we couldn't deny the magnificence of the life growing all around us, the land that supports us, or the sky that inspires awe and wonder as the stars appear one by one against a black canvas, night after night. Even if we aren't particularly "outdoorsy," nature touches our lives daily through the food we eat, the water we drink, and the sun that wakes us up and lights our way.

Our Maker clearly intended to bless us with His creation: "God saw all that He had made, and it was very good" (Genesis 1:31 NIV). Consider this gift as you walk through difficult times. Is there anything in your surroundings that brings you comfort or points to your loving Creator? Maybe flowers remind you of His beauty, or a calm body of water brings you a sense of His peace. Just as Jesus pointed to nature to illustrate many of His parables, we too can find meaning in the creation that surrounds us. Look at a tree, growing and flourishing with strength and vibrancy, and imagine how it once started as a tiny seed. "But they delight in the law of the LORD, meditating on it day and night. They are like trees planted along the riverbank, bearing fruit each season," says Psalm 1:2–3 (NLT). This verse reminds us of God's promises for those who trust in Him. Sometimes we feel like that tiny seed, awaiting a time of nurturing and growth; other times, we feel like the tree, bearing the fruit of God's goodness in our lives. He knows that we go through different seasons, and He has even given us the seasons of the year to illustrate those transitions. Take some time today to consider His creation and how it might be speaking to you during your current season. Find comfort in knowing your Creator holds the universe in His hands.

***Lord, Your creation is marvelous.***
***Help me to see You in all You have made.***

# FEELING NUMB

*Where shall I go from your Spirit? Or where shall I flee from your presence?*

*PSALM 139:7 ESV*

Sometimes grief numbs us. It's confusing, because there's so much to feel—the sadness of loss, the love we have shared, even anger or frustration that we're having to go through this.

But our minds and hearts can remain in a state of shock as we try to process and accept what has happened. In moments when we're protecting ourselves from being overwhelmed, we need to remind ourselves that it's okay to be here. It's okay to not feel for a while. God has designed us in such a way that our feelings will return when we're ready. It's possible that we can have trouble feeling Him too. In whatever way we are used to feeling His presence, we might not have that right now. This can be upsetting and confusing because at the moment, we need Him more than ever! So, it's good to remind ourselves that God is not our feelings. They may come and go, and they may help us sense a connection with Him from time to time, but He is beyond anything we will ever feel. We can trust that even in those times of numbness, He is closer than we can imagine. This is where faith comes in. Even if we have trouble feeling motivated or inspired to pray, we can remember Jesus's words in Matthew 17:20 when He told His followers that all they needed was "faith the size of a mustard seed" (AMP) and the impossible could become possible.

If you feel stuck, wondering when you'll feel reconnected in some way, remember to take your mustard seed to your Father, tiny as it may seem. Believe that He is bringing you through, and trust His timing. Know that you *will* feel all the feelings you need to feel, including His presence. And hold on to this reassurance: "The LORD is near to all who call on Him, to all who call on Him in truth" (Psalm 145:18 NIV). Keep calling on Him, past feelings, doubts, and fears. He has never left your side.

***Lord, my feelings are in Your hands.***
***I know, no matter what,***
***that You are near.***

# THROUGH IT ALL

*Then Peter got down out of the boat, walked on the water and came toward Jesus. But when he saw the wind, he was afraid and, beginning to sink, cried out, "Lord, save me!" Immediately Jesus reached out His hand and caught him.*

*MATTHEW 14:29–31 NIV*

Have you ever found yourself wishing that the Bible would give a little more detail about something? Take this story of Peter, for example, stepping out on the water to take those first few strides toward Jesus. The Bible simply says that when Peter saw the wind, "He was afraid." But we can only imagine what that fear entailed. Maybe he heard a persistent voice in his head, saying, *See? You can't trust this Jesus after all.* Or, *who do you think you are, believing you can rise above these waves?* Maybe his mind was filled with thoughts of what lay beneath the water's surface, or how deep it was, or what a bad idea it was for him to go out to Jesus in the first place.

Whether a person like Peter journeyed beside our Savior in the flesh or someone like us walks with Him in Spirit two thousand years later, we are all prone to listening to the voice of the enemy placing doubts and fears in our minds. Let's be honest—the waters we are sometimes called to walk on can seem overwhelming, the winds can be strong, and the waves can break all around us. We may hear all kinds of reasons in our minds why we'll never make it. We know Jesus is there, and we fight to keep our eyes on Him, doing our best to trust Him in the tumult, but sometimes it just doesn't feel like enough. That's when He calls us beyond feeling, to a place we may never have been before. When we cry out, "Lord, save me!" He invites us to stand firm on His promises, which are infinitely more powerful than any wind or wave that we will face in this life. He reminds us that His presence is all we need. He's not just waiting on the water—He's with us in the boat, in every step we take, and through every struggle we will ever face.

***Lord, sometimes the wind and the waves feel so overwhelming. Please help me to hold on to Your promises, no matter what.***

# GOD'S ENDLESS PURSUIT

***God** told them,*
*"I've never quit loving you and never will.*
*Expect love, love, and more love!"*
*JEREMIAH 31:3 THE MESSAGE*

If you've ever gotten a new pet, you've likely had to exercise patience as they were getting used to your house. They may have found hiding places galore as they settled in, not quite ready to trust these humans who brought them home. You may have chased them, wanting to cuddle or offer a treat, yet they still dashed beneath the couch or into the closet. We pet owners have a lot of love to give, and we just want our furry friends to soak it up.

In the same way, when we find ourselves going through difficult times, we can struggle with trusting God's love. We may find our hearts crying out, *Why this?* or, *Why now?* We can't understand why a loving Father would allow such a struggle. It is true that we can find comfort in His Word, which promises us that He has a plan to guide us through this broken world and that all who trust in Him will experience the eternal redemption of every hurt, every loss, every disappointment we face. However, when we walk difficult journeys, it can be hard to feel the truth of that promise. We may be hidden in our despair, unaware of the ways He is reaching out to us. But the truth is, we are being endlessly pursued—in both the tough and the good times. He longs to draw us near and bring us hope, peace, and joy for the journey. He is patient with our hearts and familiar with our every doubt and fear, and He knows just how to draw us out in His time. Be encouraged today—you are the object of your Savior's affection, and He wants nothing more than for you to come to Him.

***Lord, thank You for pursuing me all my life. Thank You for never giving up on me, even when I have a hard time accepting Your love. Help me to see the ways You reach out to me and to trust You more each day.***

# GOD'S PACE

***But if we hope for what we do not see, we wait for it with patience.***
*ROMANS 8:25 ESV*

If you're familiar with school drop-off and pick-up lines or restaurant drive-throughs, you've probably happened upon a few speed bumps in your time. They're usually just little annoyances we quickly get used to, but on the off chance that someone is driving along at a dangerous speed, they definitely serve a purpose. We're so used to instant gratification—getting from point A to B smoothly, clicking on this app and being taken to that site, ordering what we need and having it delivered—that we're often caught off guard when it's time to slow down.

Waiting isn't something many of us would call "enjoyable," and there are certainly plenty of other things we can think of that we'd like to be doing instead. Yet there are times in our lives when God is clearly leading us to slow down and wait, and just like when we encounter a speed bump, it's not something we would choose to do on our own. This can happen as we're walking through times of grief, wondering when in the world we're going to feel that sense of hope and joy that we long for. It can seem so far away that we may have even forgotten how it felt. These are the times when our loving Father takes us by the hand and, for whatever reason, whispers, "Wait." Instead of becoming anxious, fearing we'll never feel those good things again, we can choose to bring our sadness and discouragement to Him, trusting that He will handle us with care. We can know that He is already working behind the scenes in our hearts to bring about our healing and restoration. We can find encouragement in His Word while we wait. Even if we don't feel like jumping up in praise, we can speak the promises we read in Scripture and allow them to lift our hearts quietly. And we can reflect on His loving words of assurance: "As a mother comforts her child, so will I comfort you" (Isaiah 66:13 NIV). God knows this is a journey, and there is no rush to feel a certain way. The more we reflect on His truth, the lighter our spirits will become.

***Lord, help me to trust Your timing.***
***I bring my whole heart to You, believing that***
***You are working in me, one day at a time.***

# THE GIFT OF MEMORY

***But Mary treasured up all these things and pondered them in her heart.***

*LUKE 2:19 NIV*

As we read the story of Jesus's birth, we come upon this verse about His mother's memories. While it's easy to imagine Mary as some sort of superhuman because of God's great purpose for her, we are reminded in Scripture what a normal life she led. Just like any mother, Mary treasured in her heart her first moments with Jesus. It's something we can all relate to in one way or another. We've all been given the gift of remembrance—certain times in our lives we've cherished with the people we love most. And in our times of loss, those memories become even more precious as they provide connections with the loved ones who are no longer with us on this earth.

As we pray for God's comfort in our grief, we can be sure that one way He puts His arms around us is through the gift of memory. When Jesus gave His life, Mary was there at the foot of the cross. She faced the journey of loss just like we all do. We can imagine how God must have comforted her as she recalled moments shared with her beloved Son.

Being able to remember is a wonderful gift to help us through our toughest days. When our loving Creator knit us together, He intentionally blessed us with the ability to remember. When grief and loss entered our broken world, it was already part of His plan to help us recall the moments we shared, the connections we created in our love for each other. He also understood that some memories would be of hard things we'd rather not experience again. Just remember, He is the God of all. Pray for those comforting moments of remembrance to shine through for you. Your Father knows just what your heart needs, and He is there to lead you through.

***Lord, thank You for Your gift of memory. Please help me to find true comfort in the precious moments I've shared with loved ones.***

"IF THERE IS SOMETHING WE NEED MORE THAN ANYTHING ELSE DURING GRIEF, IT IS A FRIEND WHO STANDS WITH US, WHO DOESN'T LEAVE US. JESUS IS THAT FRIEND."

BILLY GRAHAM

# COME AWAY

*And he said,*
*"My presence will go with you,*
*and I will give you rest."*
EXODUS 33:14 ESV

Navigating the journey of loss often entails responsibilities, interactions, and practical tasks that fall on our shoulders. It can be a busy time, and we can find ourselves looking for some much-needed moments of peace. If there are days when you find yourself overwhelmed, just remember, your heavenly Father is there to help restore you in every way. Sometimes, if we listen closely with our hearts, we can hear Him drawing us away for some quiet time with Him. This may take some hard-to-find energy and motivation on our part, but we can be sure that if He is calling us away, He will make a way. It may be setting aside part of a day for us to spend in a space that inspires us to connect with Him. It could be an overnight filled with whatever relaxes us and brings us peace. However it looks for you, our good God honors those steps we take toward Him. When we trust Him with our hearts—when we tell Him, *Lord, this is overwhelming, but I know*

*You are here to carry me through*—He is surely delighted by our dependence on Him and will meet us where we are.

Jesus, in His fully human experience, knew the necessity of retreats. Mark's Gospel tells us how He sought to be alone with His Father: "And rising very early in the morning, while it was still dark, he departed and went out to a desolate place, and there he prayed" (Mark 1:35 ESV). Later, He invited His disciples to come away with Him: "The apostles returned to Jesus from their ministry tour and told Him all they had done and taught. Then Jesus said, 'Let's go off by ourselves to a quiet place and rest awhile'" (Mark 6:30–31 NLT). Sometimes it's tough to give ourselves permission to set aside quiet time, but when we do, we can discover God's life-giving love in a special way. May you always hear His invitation to find peace in His presence.

***Lord, help me to find rest in You when I need it most. You are my peace.***

# WONDERFULLY MADE

*Yet you, Lord, are our Father.*
*We are the clay, You are the potter;*
*we are all the work of Your hand.*
*ISAIAH 64:8 NIV*

One of the first things many of us learned about God when we were children is that we are each uniquely created by Him. And just as no two fingerprints are alike, no two souls are alike; He chose to cover this earth with every human imaginable, knitting us together so intentionally and intricately. However, living in a time when social media rules so many of our interactions, we can easily fall prey to the comparison game. Being a unique creation can be overshadowed by who we're *supposed* to be, what we *should* be doing, how we *ought* to be acting. . .you know how it goes.

It's important when we go through times of grief that we remember our uniqueness and avoid comparison. There are certain ways we'll feel and certain things we'll do that may never happen for someone else—because everyone grieves in their own way, in their own time. Allowing yourself the freedom of that expression is a wonderful form of self-care. Sometimes you may be surprised by your feelings or actions, and that's okay. God guides us through each journey differently but offers Himself as a steady anchor for each of us to cling to, no matter what we face. And remembering how deeply He understands us helps when it feels impossible to explain ourselves to yet another person. Of course it's a blessing to have caring friends with listening ears, but there are some things we need to reserve for our heart-to-heart times with Him. We can bring every question, every disappointment, every confusing feeling to Him and trust that He will help us sort through all of them. He will cover our entire experience with His love, and we don't have to feel lost; He will be our shelter for as long as we need. Remember the words of Psalm 139:13–14: "For You created my inmost being; You knit me together in my mother's womb. I praise You because I am fearfully and wonderfully made" (NIV). He made you one of a kind. This is your journey, and you will walk it in your own way, but you will never be alone.

***Lord, what a gift it is to be Your unique creation. Remind me that this is my own journey to walk with You.***

# SPIRITUAL SHOES

*The grass withers and the flowers fade,*
*but the word of our God stands forever.*
*ISAIAH 40:8 NLT*

Think back to your childhood for a moment. Do you remember running barefoot through the house or the front yard without a care in the world? Or maybe there's a little one in your life today who does that very thing. Kids aren't famous for taking precautions; they're just enjoying the moment, and who cares whether that involves shoes or not?

Now imagine going on a hike—leaving behind the familiar and venturing out into the woods. Would childhood-you be instructed to cover your feet? Wouldn't you stop your own child or grandchild today, reminding them to lace up their shoes because they're headed into unfamiliar territory? In the same way, we can get comfortable with the barefoot business-as-usual in our lives. Familiar tasks, familiar feelings, even a familiar connection with God each day. We know our way around, and surprises or struggles aren't welcome. But what happens on the tough trails and in the hard times? We need a covering, and God stands ready to provide it through His Word. He has given us all we need to meet any obstacle, to deal with any discouragement, to rise above any despair. As the psalmist reminds us, "Your word is a lamp to guide my feet and a light for my path" (Psalm 119:105 NLT).

The more of that Word we take in, the more protection we will have from the rocks and thorns that await us on this journey. Of course, there is much to feel and overcome, but we are free from lasting hurt; we don't have to surrender to the struggle; we can find refuge among God's promises; we can know that this path—tough as it is—leads to Life, because He goes before us.

Consider challenging yourself to spend some time in God's Word each day. Look up His specific promises and remember they are a part of His love letter to you and the world He created. Be encouraged, even if the road is rough right now; He is here to light your way and soften your path. May you sense His presence today.

*Lord, thank You for the gift of Your Word.*
*May I hold tight to all Your promises.*

# THE DOMINO EFFECT

***Be strong and take heart,***
***all you who hope in the Lord.***
*PSALM 31:24 NIV*

We've all seen what happens when someone stands a bunch of dominoes on end, creating a long line in order to knock them all over, and then sets the line in motion. It starts with a tiny nudge of that first piece, and then one by one, they fall until there are none left standing. This is a good picture of how we can feel when we're struggling to find hope in our lives. That first falling domino may be a sense of discouragement, a sad memory, or a moment of doubt—anything that weighs our hearts down and clouds our minds with negative thoughts. What can happen next is just like a line of dominoes set in motion—a chain reaction leads to feelings of despair. Once our thinking is headed in a particular direction, it can be hard to make a turnaround. Because God knows this about us, He has provided us with ways to find freedom from the negativity and find hope in Him. When we feel powerless over our domino-like thoughts and feelings, He is the One who can stop the falling and start something new.

When we recognize dark thoughts, the most important thing we can do is say, "Lord, help!" We can acknowledge that He is infinitely greater than our thoughts or feelings, and He is able to guide us toward the light. He invites us to believe in His power to change what we believe is out of our control. "Commit everything you do to the Lord. Trust Him to help you do it, and He will" (Psalm 37:5 TLB). This includes renewing our minds.

During the times in our lives when hopelessness threatens to keep us down, let us remember that He offers hope in any moment. He stands ready to stop that domino effect of our struggles anytime we turn to Him. He delights in making room for His joy and peace to rise up in our lives. Even if we barely recognize it today, the more we trust Him, the more we will sense Him bringing light into the darkness—something He has done since the beginning of time.

***Lord, help me to turn to You when negative thoughts and feelings bring me down. You are my hope!***

# EVERYDAY AWARENESS

***You make known to me the path of life;***
***in your presence there is fullness of joy.***
*PSALM 16:11 ESV*

*The Practice of the Presence of God* is a book of collected teachings by seventeenth-century monk Brother Lawrence, who had a special, everyday way of connecting with God. Through the years, his words have inspired Jesus lovers around the world to simplify their faith and live humbly with their Maker. Brother Lawrence said his faith consisted of "speaking humbly and conversing lovingly with Him all the time, at every moment, without rule or measures." The monk was known especially for making mundane tasks sacred, simply by turning his heart toward God at all times. This may not seem imaginable for some of us in the busy world we inhabit, but the idea is that this practice can truly help us in our times of grief.

Here's how it works: Our minds tend to wander, and especially when we're walking through a tough season, our thoughts can bring us down. Whether we're doing laundry, wandering through the grocery store aisles, or even talking with a friend, our focus can be on our sadness, and we can find ourselves just going through the motions. At these moments, it's good to ask ourselves, *How aware of God's presence am I right now?* Just as Brother Lawrence described, it doesn't take much but a turning of our hearts toward Him.

Walking through life with our Creator can help to lighten our spirits and give us a hope-filled outlook. It reminds us that nothing we do is meaningless—and that God cares about it all. It may take a while to remember Him in all the little things we experience in a day, but the more we do, the more peace we'll know. "For He himself is our peace," says Ephesians 2:14 (NIV), which speaks of Jesus, our forever-connector with the Father. We can make a habit of conversing with Him in our everyday moments and take comfort in how that connection shines through all we do.

***Lord, thank You that You are always with us, even in the everyday things. Help me to be more aware of Your presence each day.***

# FAITHFUL COMPANIONS

***Therefore encourage one another and build each other up, just as in fact you are doing.***
*I THESSALONIANS 5:11 NIV*

When we go through times of loss, people often reach out to ask what they can do. Offering to pray for us, bring us meals, give us help with everyday tasks—whatever we might need to keep functioning as we navigate this difficult journey. When someone asks us, "What can I do?" there is something we can always ask for, whether it's from someone who has offered to help or from someone in our lives we just know will be there for us. We can ask for them to check in with us from time to time to see how we are doing. This may sound like a silly request, because there are likely lots of people checking in on us. But it's so important to identify a few people we can be truly vulnerable with, people we can count on to make sure we're walking this path with the truth of God's Word to guide us and the hope of the Holy Spirit to keep us going.

We all have vulnerabilities, and grief can bring to

the forefront those things we struggle with. Whether we are isolating ourselves or giving in to the negative chatter that says we will never find joy again, God has His ways of leading us through the muck, and often He uses those people in our lives who know Him and can point us toward Him in our toughest moments.

Peter, in a letter to his fellow believers, reminded them that they have an enemy that seeks to bring them down. He told them to stand firm in the faith, encouraging them with these words: "And the God of all grace, who called you to His eternal glory in Christ, after you have suffered a little while, will Himself restore you and make you strong, firm and steadfast" (I Peter 5:10 NIV). We need these reminders. We need those willing souls who will stand firm with us and offer us hope on rough days. Consider reaching out to a few, just to have them in your corner. You'll be grateful to have their presence on the journey.

***Lord, help me to identify those who can walk with me and keep me pointed toward You.***

# NO REGRETS

***Now may the God of hope fill you with all joy and peace in believing, that you may abound in hope by the power of the Holy Spirit.***

***ROMANS 15:13 NKJV***

One of the things Jesus stands ready to free us from during times of loss is the feeling of regret. We all have things we wish we'd done or said, ways we wish things would've gone, or time we wish we'd used better while we had it. The enemy has a way of bringing up the past in a negative light, trying to get us to blame ourselves and live with the *would'ves*, *could'ves*, and *should'ves*. It's so important that we recognize that voice and realize it's not coming from our Father. God is always inviting us toward light, and hope, and goodness. His love shines into our darkest moments, and He inspires us to lift our heads and find peace in His presence. One way we can do this is by inviting happy memories into our minds as often as we can. Ask Him to remind you of the good times and reflect on the blessings you shared. You can also ask Him to help you look forward with hope that your heart is healing, day by day.

The Bible is filled with people who could've had

all kinds of regrets, but Jesus showed them a different way. “One thing I do,” said Paul, “forgetting those things which are behind and reaching forward to those things which are ahead” (Philippians 3:13 NKJV). From the moment of your loss, God has been working for your restoration. Yes, it takes time, but you can always trust that He is moving you forward, helping you let go of the negative and focus on the positive.

So, when that voice of regret tries to move in, remember that it’s no longer yours to deal with. “But the Lord is faithful,” said Paul in II Thessalonians 3:3. “He will establish you and guard you against the evil one” (ESV). It takes practice, but the more you resist regret and allow God to replace your darker thoughts with good things, the lighter you will feel.

***Lord, please bless my memories, and help me to look forward with hope.***

# TIME AND SPACE

*The Lord is my shepherd, I lack nothing.*
*He makes me lie down in green pastures,*
*He leads me beside quiet waters,*
*He refreshes my soul.*
*PSALM 23:1–3 NIV*

We expect a lot of ourselves—have you ever thought about that? Whether it's doing our job, or parenting, or even being a good church member or citizen in the community, we often have full calendars and great ideations. But when we're hit with a season of grief, it can feel quite overwhelming to keep up with everything. We're so used to being the one who shows up, says "yes," makes the plan, or answers the call. It's hard when we need to step back or bow out.

David's words of refreshment in Psalm 23 can speak to our hearts especially in this time. God, who knows the depth of our hurt and the magnitude of our struggle, has a way of calling us into stillness and rest. As we sense that call, we can give ourselves permission to lower our expectations and shorten our to-do lists as much as we need. We can allow others to step up and provide, knowing that we, too, will be there for them in their toughest times. Our own seasons of brokenness—those times when our hearts are raw and we need nurturing and care—those are the times when our loving Father longs to draw us extra close to Him. We need unhurried time and sacred quiet for Him to speak comfort and peace to us.

How about you? Are your expectations high, or have you been able to let go and allow yourself the time and space you need? Do you see yourself as having just as much worth when you are not "doing" as when your plate is full? You are precious to God no matter what your plans are. Imagine how delighted He is when you are able to slow down and rest in His presence. If that's all you are able to do today, it is more than enough.

***Lord, thank You for Your comforting, loving presence. Remind me often to slow down and receive all You have for me during this season of my life.***

# GOD'S TRUTH

***Every word of God proves true.
He is a shield to all who come to Him
for protection.***
***PROVERBS 30:5 NLT***

When it comes to Bible stories, Job's is a tough one to read. His struggles seem endless, and it can be discouraging to wonder why God would allow someone to go through so much. But one thing his story brings to light is the importance of hearing from God and not being swayed by the words of others who may not offer the best advice.

During his difficult journey, Job had three friends who came forward to give him their suggestions. It turns out that their words were more harmful than helpful—they were not based on God's truth but on human assumptions. This is a good reminder for us as we experience our own times of loss. There are often many people who try to encourage us, give us advice, or even share their opinions about how God is involved in all of it. Many of them are well-meaning friends or family members who just want to help us in our hurt. But it's so important that we receive the words of others through the filter of the Holy Spirit. We need time to grieve, and that's something people don't understand sometimes. Even Jesus grieved. There are lots of examples in God's Word of those who mourned the loss of their loved ones for a long time. It was a while before they were ready to hear cheerful words of encouragement or to be reminded that God will work all things for their good.

God is absolutely working to redeem our tough times, but sometimes we need to discover this for ourselves. We may have loved ones who want to share sources of comfort, hope, and joy, but our greatest healing will come as we keep ourselves focused on His redeeming love. His Word reminds us that He is the reason we have hope, no matter what we face: "Yes, my soul, find rest in God; my hope comes from Him" (Psalm 62:5–6 NIV). Helpful words are always welcome—this is just a gentle reminder to consider His truth above all.

*Lord, thank You for Your Word.*
*Help me to consider Your truth over everything.*

# HELD TOGETHER

***And he took them in his arms and blessed them, laying his hands on them.***

*MARK 10:16 ESV*

Some days it's okay to fall apart. It doesn't mean God's not with us, or we've given up, or we've lost our way. It just means our human selves have some letting go to do. This can be hard for a lot of us. We may feel we need permission to fall apart, but no one has given it to us. We may be trying to keep it together for others who need us to be strong. We may believe our faith is weak if we allow ourselves to cry out in desperation, or confusion, or fear. But that's not the case at all. Honesty with God is always the first step to intimacy. He wants us to bring our brokenness to Him. As we do, we are reminded that we are only falling apart into His presence. We are securely surrounded by His love. Whatever we need to speak, however the tears flow or the cries come, they are held in His infinite heart for us.

As Paul said in Acts 17:28, "For in Him we live and move and have our being" (NIV). We can't fall far enough or doubt deeply enough or despair long enough to leave His presence. We rest eternally in His arms. Days like this can be a good time to imagine Jesus beside us, holding us in the most comforting hug imaginable. Remember, there's no safer place to be. "Christ is the visible image of the invisible God. He existed before anything was created and is supreme over all creation. . . Everything was created through Him and for Him. He existed before anything else, and He holds all creation together" (Colossians 1:15–17 NLT). We are in good hands on those fall-apart days. Jesus deeply understands every feeling, welcomes us just as we are, and offers comfort in just the way and just the time we need. Sometimes these moments of falling apart are necessary, but we can always look forward to new mornings and brighter days ahead.

***Lord, help me remember that***
***it's okay to fall apart into Your arms.***
***Thank You for Your constant, comforting presence.***

"GRIEF IS
IN TWO PARTS.
THE FIRST IS LOSS.
THE SECOND IS
IN THE REMAKING
OF LIFE."

ANNE ROIPHE

# FREEDOM FROM FEAR

*When I am afraid,*
*I put my trust in you.*
*PSALM 56:3 ESV*

Fear is something many of us will experience on this journey, and it takes on lots of forms. We may struggle with anxiety about facing another day, wondering how we will make it through. We may worry that we'll never feel true joy or peace again. We may be afraid of facing another loss—something we just can't imagine living through right now. A lot can come against us in this time of vulnerability, and it can become a burden we just get used to bearing. It's good to remember that our loving Father invites us into freedom from fear. Scripture reminds us over and over to bring what we're carrying to Him and to practice trusting Him with our future—whether that be ten minutes or ten years from now—because He holds it all.

The enemy of our souls wants nothing more than to darken our days with "what-ifs" and to keep us from walking in the light of faith God has given us, but because that enemy has been defeated, we are free from his lies. However, we have to remind ourselves of that daily. It's good to check in with our thoughts regularly, to ask ourselves, *What is weighing me down right now?* or, *What fears am I carrying?* We can then name those things and bring them to God, who waits patiently to take them from us. We can even envision ourselves putting every fearful thought into His hands and feel a sense of lightness as we release them.

Psalm 34:4 encourages us: "I sought the Lord, and He answered me; He delivered me from all my fears" (NIV). Not just a few of those fears but *all*. Even if you have to remind yourself of this several times a day for a while, don't give up. Sometimes these truths need time to make their way from our heads to our hearts.

***Lord, I bring my worry and anxiety to You today. I trust You to free me from all my fear.***

# WATER TO WINE

*And to know this love that surpasses knowledge—*
*that you may be filled to the measure*
*of all the fullness of God.*
*EPHESIANS 3:19 NIV*

You may have read about Jesus's first recorded miracle performed at a wedding in Cana in Galilee. They had run out of wine at the great feast, and when Jesus's mother told Him, He did something about it: "Nearby stood six stone water jars, the kind used by the Jews for ceremonial washing, each holding from twenty to thirty gallons. Jesus said to the servants, 'Fill the jars with water'; so they filled them to the brim. Then He told them, 'Now draw some out and take it to the master of the banquet.' They did so, and the master of the banquet tasted the water that had been turned into wine" (John 2:6–9 NIV). The master praised the bridegroom for the good wine, not knowing where it had come from.

Let's imagine that we are the ones in this story who have run out of something. Losing someone precious to us can make us feel empty inside, like those stone water jars. The space that person once filled in our lives is now unoccupied, and this can make us feel very lonely. It is true that no one can ever fill their shoes; that's something we must face as we grieve. But Jesus stands ready to fill those places with His comfort and peace if we will turn our hearts toward Him in our sadness. Just as He instructed the servants to fill those jars with water, He asks us to bring Him the water of our faith. It's not a feeling—it's a choice to believe that He is with us and that He can heal us in His time. There will be a day when we look back and realize He has taken our jars of water and turned them into wine. He will replace our doubt with hope, our fear with peace, our loneliness with comfort—one day at a time. All He asks is that we trust Him and look to Him, and He will do the rest. May you sense the fullness of His love today.

***Lord, strengthen my faith and fill me with Your love, all the days of my life.***

# CALLED TOGETHER

*But if we walk in the light,*
*as He is in the light,*
*we have fellowship with one another.*
*1 JOHN 1:7 NIV*

When Jesus called His disciples, one by one, He surely had in mind the kind of community they would create. After all, He was inviting them out of the world—to live a new kind of life with new priorities, beliefs, and experiences. He knew they would do life together, and it would be different than the lives they'd lived with others. They'd connect differently, celebrate differently, grieve differently—the Kingdom of God would turn their world upside down in a way, but they would also come to understand each other deeply, because they were all in it together.

Fast-forward to today. We, too, are called to live in community. We, too, are called to point each other to the One who created our hearts and knows exactly what we need. We, too, are called to listen to each other, learn from each other, study God's Word with each other. And when hard times come, we are called to walk alongside each other, reminding each other to "set your minds on things above, not on earthly things" (Colossians 3:2 NIV). We stand on God's promises together, pray together, and discuss our doubts with each other with vulnerability and openness. Even though we may be tempted to isolate ourselves in times of sadness, it is good to remember that we are part of a beautiful community. When Jesus called us—just like He called the disciples—He knew what we would go through and experience together. Because of His love, we will never walk alone.

*Lord, thank You for the community You have given me. Help me to connect with others on the journey to experience Your healing love.*

# THE GIFT OF GRATITUDE

*Give thanks in all circumstances;*
*for this is the will of God in Christ Jesus for you.*
*I THESSALONIANS 5:18 ESV*

Being grateful is definitely easier in some seasons than others. And God's Word reminds us that no matter what experience we are having, we are called to give thanks. Of course, we may not be giving thanks *for* our circumstances, but we can find ways to be grateful *in the midst of* them. God knows that when our hearts are lifted in gratitude, our spirits are lightened, and we can experience a heavenly connection; He inhabits our praise. This isn't just a Christian belief; modern psychology argues that finding ways to be thankful is a major step toward positive mental health. But we who follow Jesus have the wonderful blessing of knowing *who* to thank!

When you're dealing with those "down" days and needing some encouragement, consider starting a gratitude list. Grab a journal or your laptop, or open that memo app on your phone, and just begin with a few simple things that have brought you joy. It could be your family, or the fact that you have a warm home, or a favorite cup of coffee. As you walk through your day, try to pay attention to those everyday gifts that appear and take a moment to write them down. Pretty soon, you'll have a whole collection of reasons to say, "Thank You, Lord" as you find yourself blessed with glimmers of joy. This could be something you choose to do for one day, or maybe you make it a habit and get used to looking daily for those simple things that God provides to make you smile. That's one wonderful thing about Him—nothing is too small for Him to use in your life. As you pray for brighter days ahead, know that He answers in all kinds of ways. The more you are able to lift your heart in gratitude for the little things, the more you will see Him reaching out to you in ways that only He can.

*Lord, help me to see all the ways*
*You bless me in my days.*
*Thank You for the gift of gratitude!*

# LIVING WATER

*"I am the Alpha and the Omega,*
*the Beginning and the End.*
*To the thirsty I will give water without cost*
*from the spring of the water of life."*
*REVELATION 21:6 NIV*

It seems like everyone has a favorite water bottle or cup these days. People of all ages like to keep their water containers full and nearby so they can take a swig anytime. There's just something about knowing it's there if we need it—about knowing we never have to worry about being thirsty—that brings a sense of comfort. It's no wonder that God is associated with water throughout His Word. When we feel disconnected from Him or find ourselves in a dark place, we can feel spiritually dry. As the psalmist declared: "O God, you are my God; earnestly I seek you; my soul thirsts for you; my flesh faints for you, as in a dry and weary land where there is no water" (Psalm 63:1 ESV). God makes it clear throughout Scripture that He intends to quench our thirst—to be that consistent Source of Life we need to thrive throughout our days. However, our seasons of loss can find us running on empty. Let us try to remember that He hasn't gone anywhere—we may just be struggling to sense His presence with us.

The most life-giving thing we can do in these tough times is to allow ourselves to be filled up again. That looks different for each of us. How about you? What are some things that give you a sense of closeness with Him? For some, it's listening to music. For others, it's taking a nature walk. Still others reach for a prayer journal or set aside a moment of the day for some quiet time with His Word in their favorite space. Whatever you do, just think—you are connecting with the Creator of the universe. He has so much to pour into you. It's His desire to constantly refresh you: "The LORD will guide you continually, giving you water when you are dry and restoring your strength. You will be like a well-watered garden, like an ever-flowing spring" (Isaiah 58:11 NLT). Anytime you feel dry, seek Him out, and know He is waiting full of love to provide all you need.

*Lord, You are our Living Water.*
*May I be filled in Your Presence today.*

# OUR QUESTIONS

***"For just as the heavens are higher than the earth, so My ways are higher than your ways and My thoughts higher than your thoughts."***

*ISAIAH 55:9 NLT*

We all know what it's like to ask God "Why?" *Why do these things have to happen? Why do I still feel this way? Why can't I just know Your peace and joy again? Why can't I sense Your presence right now?* Being the patient and compassionate Creator that He is, we can count on Him to love us through every question we can muster. We may not, however, find answers to our questions right away. But we can trust that all our wondering matters to Him, and that He will be faithful in showing us truths that help us put our questions to rest.

Meanwhile, here's the most important thing we can do as we wonder: *we can choose to trust Him*. We're in good company here, as God's people—those who have faced struggles, seemingly impossible situations, or temptations to just give up—have been asked to do the same thing for thousands of years. He invites us in all sorts of ways to trust Him in the midst of it all, even when we don't understand it. And He never leaves His people stuck in their questioning. He leads them forward and helps them to see the bigger picture as time passes, and He can do the same for you.

It's true that on this side of heaven, not everything will make sense. But trusting that God holds our entire lives in His hands helps us to loosen our grip on needing all the answers. Paul's reminder can help us to understand and have hope: "Now we see things imperfectly, like puzzling reflections in a mirror, but then we will see everything with perfect clarity. All that I know now is partial and incomplete, but then I will know everything completely, just as God now knows me completely" (I Corinthians 13:12 NLT). Remember, our Father welcomes our questions and holds us in our struggles. He offers us the truth of His Word to help bring peace to our minds, and the more we trust Him, the more assurance we will feel.

***Lord, help me to trust You,***
***even when I don't understand everything.***
***I know You hold my life in Your hands.***

# HERE, AMONG US

*Jesus told her,*
*"I am the resurrection and the life."*
*JOHN 11:25 NLT*

While there's one time each year that we focus on Jesus's world-changing resurrection, it's something we can choose to think about daily—especially in life's greatest challenges. Whether we're dealing with sadness or discouragement or we're just plain exhausted, we need that life-giving reminder that none of these things will have the last word. Whatever bit of darkness is trying to creep into our lives, there is a Savior shining a brighter light. There is One who is showing us, *I took this. I beat this. It is not yours to carry anymore.* Of course, we all heal at our own pace, but when we truly realize what's been won for us, it sets us on that firm path of hope. "And this hope will not lead to disappointment. For we know how dearly God loves us, because He has given us the Holy Spirit to fill our hearts with His love" (Romans 5:5 NLT).

You may have heard of the Road to Emmaus, where two of Jesus's disciples were walking after His death and resurrection. Jesus showed up among them as an unrecognizable man and asked them, "What are you discussing together as you walk along?" (Luke 24:17 NIV). "'About Jesus of Nazareth,' they replied. 'He was a prophet, powerful in word and deed'" (Luke 24:19 NIV). They continued to tell Him all about what had just happened. Then, still unrecognizable to the disciples, Jesus explained to them all that was written in the Scriptures concerning Himself—how He had fulfilled everything. It wasn't until they reached their destination and broke bread together that their eyes were opened to who He truly was—the resurrected Christ—and He disappeared from sight. As they remembered the experience, they asked each other, "Were not our hearts burning within us?" (Luke 24:32 NIV). His presence was undeniable. We, too, can experience Him in our own ways and not even be aware of it. Let us ask God to open our eyes and hearts to His hopeful guidance in our daily lives.

*Lord, You are the risen One!*
*Help me to see You everywhere.*

# TODAY'S WEATHER

***"I will make a pathway through the wilderness. I will create rivers in the dry wasteland."***

*ISAIAH 43:19 NLT*

If you happen to live in a place where the weather is nice year-round, you're probably not used to radical changes. You may have endured some thundershowers and some warmer-than-usual days, but you know there are people across the globe who have faced violent ice storms, flash floods, and scorching heat—sometimes without any warning. Weather forecasters can do their best to predict what will happen in our environment, but in the end, we who live in those places are left to face whatever creation has to offer at the moment. In the same way, those milder times in our lives can bring good expectations; our inner climate may be favorable, and we don't find ourselves worried about what the next day will bring. We may have a business-as-usual routine that works for us, and we're grateful when nothing gets in the way of that. But the tough times? That's when the unforeseen weather shows up inside us. It's stormy in our spirits, and we may be asking God, *When will the sun shine for me again?*

Our feelings are unpredictable; we may be doing well one day and get hit out of nowhere with the tough stuff the next. Remember that just because we're struggling today, it doesn't mean that tomorrow is hopeless. God knows our feelings intimately; Jesus felt them all. We can bring Him our bad weather days and trust that He can bring something good from them. It may seem impossible in the moment, but making things possible is our Father's specialty. No matter what you're facing today, He invites you to bring every disturbing thought, every disheartening feeling, to Him. Lay it all down and trust that He is working through it all for your redemption. You may not experience the results immediately, but if you pay attention to your circumstances and the people around you, you will see His hand at work. If you take the time to read His encouraging words in Scripture, they will help bring lighter days too. Don't listen to the lie of the enemy that says you're stuck in a storm. Keep your eyes on Jesus, friend, and let Him lead You into brighter tomorrows.

***Lord, some days are tough, and I need extra encouragement to believe better times will come. Thank You for always being my Light.***

# HIS GOOD WORK

*And I am certain that God,*
*who began the good work within you,*
*will continue His work until it is finally finished*
*on the day when Christ Jesus returns.*
*PHILIPPIANS 1:6 NLT*

At some point, we learn that becoming more like Jesus is a lifelong process. There are times when it is more evident that God is working in us, and those times are so encouraging. We may recall seasons of unexplainable peace and joy, and how wonderful it can be to know where those things truly come from. We may have experienced His transformation in healed relationships, a greater capacity for grace, or a growing desire to serve others. There are so many reasons to be thankful for the ways He is at work in our lives. The most difficult seasons, however, are often when He does His deepest work, and it just plain hurts sometimes.

Right now, we may only see the tough day ahead of us, but He sees who we are becoming in the long run. He has had plans to turn our darkness to light before we ever knew His name. Sometimes, though, it feels like all we have to hold on to is trust—trust that His heart is good, trust that He is *for* us, trust that He is using every little detail of our lives to write a beautiful story that reaches into eternity.

Often, our hurt is so deep that it's impossible to imagine what He's up to within us. We are just trying to make it through the day in survival mode; that sense of peace and joy we once knew seems like a dream. One thing we can do to find encouragement in the most difficult times is to ask, *Lord, please show me how You're working in me.* As we become more aware of the changes He's making and the ways He's guiding us, we can find hope that this time of our lives has purpose. As hard as it is, it isn't meaningless, and one day we will look back to see all He did to help us follow more closely in the footsteps of our precious Savior.

***Lord, thank You for working in me***
***to make me more like Jesus.***
***Help me to trust in You each day.***

# INSIDE AND OUT

***You have searched me, Lord,***
***and You know me.***
*PSALM 139:1 NIV*

What a gift it is to learn that we are fully known by our God! Remember the Samaritan woman Jesus encountered at the well? He revealed this beautiful truth to her one sunny afternoon. First, He let her know that He was offering her more than the plain old water she had come to draw; He spoke to her of Living Water—the kind that never ends, the kind that gives us eternal life. "The woman said to Him, 'Sir, give me this water so that I won't get thirsty and have to keep coming here to draw water.' He told her, 'Go, call your husband and come back.' 'I have no husband,' she replied. Jesus said to her, 'You are right when you say you have no husband. The fact is, you have had five husbands, and the man you now have is not your husband. What you have just said is quite true'" (John 4:15–18 NIV). She marveled at the fact that He somehow *knew* her completely, and soon, she was sharing it with everyone: "Then, leaving her water jar, the woman went back to the town and said to the people, 'Come, see a man who told me everything I ever did. Could this be the Messiah?'" (John 4:28–29 NIV).

This is our Jesus—the One who knows us inside and out, the One we don't have to take the time to explain ourselves to, the One who understands before we even try to put anything into words. Going through difficult times can make us feel alone in our struggles, and we may find ourselves wishing that others could really "get" how we are feeling. Maybe we don't feel like explaining it for the hundredth time; maybe we're tired of feeling misunderstood. Let us always remember that Jesus sees us, knows us thoroughly, and loves us just as we are. And He is always waiting for us to bring our whole selves to Him, so that He can provide exactly what we need. May you have that comforting sense of being known and understood today.

***Lord, please remind me every day of the beautiful truth that I am fully known and understood by You.***

"THERE IS NOTHING WRONG WITH FALLING AT THE FEET OF JESUS IN SILENCE. GOD CAN HEAR YOUR TEARS, HE KNOWS YOUR HEART, HE KNOWS YOU. YOU DON'T ALWAYS HAVE TO SPEAK."

STASI ELDREDGE

# CARING FOR OURSELVES

*What is man that you are mindful of him,*
*and the son of man that you care for him?*
*Yet you have made him a little lower than the heavenly*
*beings and crowned him with glory and honor.*

*PSALM 8:4–5 ESV*

If there's ever been a time to give yourself grace and compassion and understanding, consider that the time to do this is now. If we can imagine that these things flow from God's heart to ours in our most difficult times, we can believe they are within us to draw from. This isn't something a lot of us are used to, because we can be so hard on ourselves. We may not struggle to show *others* God's love, but what about ourselves? His love comes to us in so many ways, but one way it comes to us is *through* us. We are His treasures. He *wants* us to care for ourselves, to treat ourselves with the kindness He offers, to know our great worth in Jesus.

A season of loss opens the door to a lot of need in our lives, and one of the most loving things we can do for ourselves is to ask for what we need. It may be a moment alone, or it may be the comfort of company. We may be struggling with the well-meaning advice and encouragement that others have to share right now, and it's okay to let them know we need a break. We may need prayer—don't be afraid to post that request or come forward in a church service or call on those you know will lift you up. We may need constant reminders that it's going to be okay. Ask for assurance from friends and family members; many of them are just waiting to help in some way but don't know how. If you've had offers for practical help around the house, with childcare, with meals, or at work. . .take them! Give yourself whatever breaks you can, and don't feel guilty. It's a blessing for others to bless you. If you don't know what you need right now, consider asking God to help you identify it. Remember, as your loving Father, He cares deeply about how you experience this journey. He wants you to be loved and cared for through it all and can provide many ways to make that happen.

*Lord, help me to care*
*for myself in the days to come.*
*Thank You for providing for all my needs.*

# THE GIFT OF LOVE

***Beloved, let us love one another, for love is from God, and whoever loves has been born of God and knows God.***

*I JOHN 4:7 ESV*

Have you ever just paused to thank God for the privilege of being able to love? It's something we might not think of on the darker days we go through, but when we're able to come up for air, it's a miraculous thing to ponder. Our God, who is love *Himself*, gave us the chance to experience that love with one another. We hurt so much in these times of loss because we've loved so deeply. But Jesus reminds us again and again that His love goes where no human love has gone. When we find ourselves struggling with the pain of loss, we can remember that love still fills our lives. It comes from everywhere—from those who walk alongside us, from those who lift us up in prayer, even from those who call and don't know what to say but reach out anyway to let us know they care. Love is forever changing forms, and God is forever revealing it to us in His own unique way.

Part of grieving is realizing we can't connect with our dear ones in the ways we used to. However, our love for them lives on, and we can be sure that our gracious Father will guide us in finding that place in our hearts for it to remain. Meanwhile, His love brings us hope and grace and goodness and light in the darkness. He wants it to fill our empty places, lift us up when we feel defeated, and pour through us to those who need to know who He truly is. During the highs and lows of this journey, don't forget the love you've been blessed to carry in your heart. Remember the constant love of God, there for you every day and every night, drawing you closer to Him, preparing you for that beautiful day when you will see Him face-to-face.

*Lord, thank You for the privilege of loving.*
*May I receive all the love You have for me today.*

# DRAWING CLOSER TO HIM

*For I can do everything through Christ,*
*who gives me strength.*
*PHILIPPIANS 4:13 NLT*

No one likes to feel needy. In fact, many of us spend quite a bit of time and energy just to ensure that we're on top of things, that we have all the answers, that we don't have to ask for help. And this can work well in seasons when things seem to be going our way. Sometimes we even become so dependent on our own strength that we forget the One who provides everything we need. But then life brings the hard stuff, and we're left feeling helpless. Those things that kept us going—the mountains we conquered, the recognition we earned, the ducks we had all in a row—don't hold us up anymore. Suddenly we no longer feel strong and capable; we can't imagine fighting a daily battle or claiming victory over whatever threatens to knock us down. These are the moments when our patient, compassionate Father gently reminds us that all the strength we will ever need is found in Him. And while it was never His desire that we should have to experience the pain of loss, it *is* His desire that we learn to wholly lean on Him for everything we walk through in this life. The more we turn to Him in this time of need, the closer to Him we will become. What we see as a time of weakness, He sees as a time to draw us in—to invite us to experience Him in deeper ways.

As Isaiah 41:10 reminds us, "Fear not, for I am with you; be not dismayed, for I am your God; I will strengthen you, yes, I will help you, I will uphold you with My righteous right hand" (NKJV). How does He strengthen us? One prayer at a time, one day at a time. There is no doubt that we will look back on these unimaginably hard times and see how they changed us. It is possible that we will learn to rely more and more on our God, not only during our tough times but during *all* our times. We will learn to see how near He really is, every day of our lives.

***Lord, You are my strength!***
***Draw me close to You each day and***
***remind me that You are all I need.***

# HOLDING ON

*But He was pierced for our transgressions,*
*He was crushed for our iniquities;*
*the punishment that brought us peace was on Him,*
*and by His wounds we are healed.*

*ISAIAH 53:5 NIV*

Times of loss can feel so uncertain. It can seem like the spiritual ground is shifting beneath us; we find ourselves wondering if we'll ever have our solid footing again; we search for something to steady us in the midst of it all. It's times like these when our heavenly Father offers us something to hold on to, that ancient symbol of His love and grace—the cross.

No matter what we face in a day, no matter how far away we feel from God or how disheartened we may be, we can return again and again to that sacrifice and victory of Jesus to re-center and renew us on this journey. When someone walks this road without Him, there is no hope—no deep comfort amid the sadness. But when we, as God's children, suffer a loss, we know that our Savior is already providing for our healing. He gave Himself so that the brokenness of the world wouldn't have the last say in our lives. He took on the darkness so that we could walk in the light—even through our most challenging seasons.

First Peter 2:24 reminds us that "by His wounds [we] have been healed" (NIV), and that includes our hearts. He absorbed the discouragement, depression, and hopelessness that would threaten to keep us down. Let us always remember that God has met us in our humanness. When we start to feel defeated, let us envision the cross and witness His healing love poured out for each of us. Carrying a cross in your pocket, on a necklace, or in some other way you might keep it close to you can be a wonderful reminder of the eternal truth you have to hold on to on those uncertain days. There's a reason you can rest in the comfort and peace of God. There's a reason you can walk with hope and assurance through even the hardest times. Your Savior is risen, and His life is yours.

***Lord, thank You for the cross.***
***Remind me daily of the healing You brought***
***through Your suffering, death, and resurrection.***

# MORE THAN ENOUGH

***Listen to my voice in the morning, Lord.
Each morning I bring my requests to
You and wait expectantly.***

*PSALM 5:3 NLT*

The world doesn't stop for us like we sometimes wish it would while we're walking the journey of grief. It can be daunting just to wake up and face a new day when we feel depleted and disconnected. We have schedules to keep, people to answer to, family to care for. The ability to press a pause button would be wonderful, but it just doesn't happen that way. We may hear or read the well-meaning words that God is with us, but in the moment, it's hard to feel the truth of that. It can feel like going through the motions, and we might wonder when we'll ever feel like ourselves again.

Consider this story of Jesus and His followers who needed enough food to feed a large crowd: "That evening the disciples came to Him and said, 'This is a remote place, and it's already getting late. Send the crowds away so they can go to the villages and buy food for themselves.' But Jesus said, 'That isn't necessary—you feed them.' 'But we have only five loaves of bread and two fish!' they answered. 'Bring them here,' He said. Then He told the people to sit down on the grass. Jesus took the five loaves and two fish, looked up toward heaven, and blessed them. Then, breaking the loaves into pieces, He gave the bread to the disciples, who distributed it to the people. They all ate as much as they wanted, and afterward, the disciples picked up twelve baskets of leftovers" (Matthew 14:15–20 NLT). The disciples saw a need through their human eyes and urged Jesus to turn the people away. They knew they didn't have enough to provide. But He knew differently. He saw in the Spirit that there was more than enough. Jesus sees you this way too. He knows what little you have to offer in your own strength right now, and He stands ready to take that offering and use it for His purposes. There is so much happening in us that we can't see. Consider beginning each day offering to Him whatever you have, and remember that He is doing powerful work behind the scenes to multiply your efforts.

***Lord, please take what little I have to offer.***
***I trust that You'll supply all I need.***

# YOUR OWN WORDS

***Gracious words are like a honeycomb,***
***sweetness to the soul and health to the body.***
***PROVERBS 16:24 ESV***

Whether you've had some good days, some rough days, or you're somewhere in between, here's an important question to consider: *How are your connections?* Are you a frequent texter, or a talk-on-the-phone type of person? Maybe you prefer a one-on-one visit, or you enjoy being with a group. Whatever you are drawn to, it's so important to stay connected in times like this. We need to know we're not alone, and even if we don't feel like it, we need to encourage ourselves to reach out. Besides those modes of communication that we're used to, there's something else we can do that doesn't happen a lot anymore—something that has brought people together for generations. We can write a letter. Does that sound unthinkable to you? We're so used to sending a sentence or two, using all our technology for quick responses; who in the world takes time to put pen to paper anymore? And yet writing a letter is a wonderful opportunity to allow ourselves to express how we truly feel. We can take our time, sitting down to tap into what's going on within and sharing it with our words.

Is there anyone in your life you feel you can be transparent with—someone you know you can trust to provide some encouragement in return? Sometimes there are things we just can't express in a text, or words we don't feel ready to say out loud. When we give ourselves time to write, we give those things time to come out. It can be such a relief to be honest about how we're doing, knowing our words will be received by a caring heart. If paper is too old-fashioned for you, try an email or whatever gives you the space to say all that comes to your mind. Remember, the New Testament is filled with precious truths we'd never have known if the authors had not sat down to pour out their hearts in their letters. Why not give it a try? Someone out there will be blessed to hear from you, and you will have the chance to let your heart speak too.

***Lord, help me to reach out and find the words to share. Thank You for the connections You've blessed me with.***

# HOLY IMAGINATION

*"Peace I leave with you; My peace I give you.*
*I do not give to you as the world gives.*
*Do not let your hearts be troubled and do not be afraid."*
*JOHN 14:27 NIV*

There are moments surrounding the loss of a loved one that we'd rather not revisit. We can be going through our day, doing okay, when suddenly something will come to mind that takes us back, brings us down, and makes us wonder if it will always be this painful. It's true that healing is a journey, and what steals our joy today may not be there tomorrow. But wherever we are in the process, there's one thing we can always do: *invite Jesus in*. Even though we know He's always been with us in everything we've gone through, we may not have been aware of it in the moment. We may have gone through times of confusion, fear, or despair, wondering why we had to face the pain of loss in our lives. But when those moments come up in our memory today, we can ask Jesus to join us in them. We can picture Him there with us, imagine His loving arms around us and

His comforting words whispered: "I will give you rest" (Matthew 11:28 NIV). The more we learn to invite Him into those memories, the more peace we will find.

How about you? Do you ever imagine Him beside you in your toughest times? We may read His Word; others may remind us of His promises; we may spend time in prayer every day, but God has given us the gift of vision for a reason. Something new happens when we choose to truly see Him in our lives. We are reminded that our faith is not wishful thinking; it's not a fairy tale or a good idea; it's the realest reality we'll ever know. Our faithful God is constantly revealing Himself to us in all kinds of ways. Next time you recall a tough moment, consider putting your holy imagination to work and see Him there with you, guarding you, holding you, and filling you with His peace.

*Lord, help me to see You*
*in my toughest moments and memories.*
*Thank You for being our peace.*

# A TIME TO WEEP

*You have kept count of my tossings;*
*put my tears in your bottle.*
*PSALM 56:8 ESV*

We experience God's gift of tears throughout our lives, both in moments of inexpressible joy and in times when our pain and sadness are beyond words. Some of us just naturally cry more than others, but no matter how often those tears flow, they are clearly messengers from our hearts, allowing us to deeply express the feelings we cannot contain.

Throughout the Bible, God makes it clear that our tears matter greatly to Him. When Jesus was called to Lazarus' home when he died, Lazarus' sister, Mary, fell at His feet in tears. John 11:33 tells us: "When Jesus saw her weeping. . .he was deeply moved in his spirit and greatly troubled" (ESV). Jesus reveals to us the heart of God. He draws near to us, especially in our sorrow, and provides healing in His time and in His way: "He heals the brokenhearted and binds up their wounds" (Psalm 147:3 ESV). He reminds us that in this broken world, there will be a time for everything: "A time to weep, and a time to laugh; a time to mourn, and a time to dance"

(Ecclesiastes 3:4 ESV). But He is never surprised by these times. He knew that our tears would come, and He already knows how He will comfort us on the journey. If we allow Him, He surely longs to draw us extra close in these times, to speak peace to our hearts, to calm our fears, and to remind us that our lives can still be filled with so much joy as we trust Him to lead us through the darker times.

Christ is our light. He is the reason that sadness will not have the last word in the lives of those who put their trust in Him. As we are reminded in the end: "He will wipe away every tear from their eyes, and death shall be no more, neither shall there be mourning, nor crying, nor pain anymore, for the former things have passed away (Revelation 21:4 ESV).

*Lord, I welcome Your gift of tears when my feelings are beyond words. Thank You for drawing close to comfort my heart.*

# SPEAK UP

*The grass withers, the flower fades,*
*but the word of our God will stand forever.*
ISAIAH 40:8 ESV

The Bible is full of reminders of how powerful words can be. After all, God created the whole universe with His words. And we are constantly cautioned to consider our words carefully, as Proverbs cautions us: "Death and life are in the power of the tongue, and those who love it will eat its fruits" (Proverbs 18:21 ESV). But during our most difficult times, we can forget the truth of that. We may be struggling with doubt or discouragement, and we can often find those frustrating feelings falling out of our mouths. It's important that we're able to express the tough things we feel, and having other trusted souls hear our words and give us a safe place to break down is a good and necessary thing. But it's also important, along with our venting, that we remember to speak words of faith and hope on our healing journey. That's where affirmations based on God's Word come in.

There's something about hearing yourself proclaim the truth that can lift your spirit and bring that wonderful sense of assurance that God is with you, and He is actively working in your life, and nothing you are going through will be wasted. You might have some favorite verses of encouragement to turn into your own affirmations. Here are some you may wish to use in addition:

- *My God will meet all my needs* (Philippians 4:19 NIV).
- *The Lord will fulfill His purpose for me* (Psalm 138:8 ESV).
- *Your comfort gives me hope and cheer* (Psalm 94:19 NLT).
- *The peace of Christ rules in my heart* (Colossians 3:15 ESV).
- *The Lord holds my hand and takes away my fear* (Isaiah 41:13 NLT).
- I *hope in the Lord and He renews my strength* (Isaiah 40:31 NIV).
- *God will restore me* (I Peter 5:10 NIV).
- *Nothing can separate me from the love of God* (Romans 8:38–39 NIV).

Consider tucking a few of these affirmations away in your heart for the days to come.

***Lord, thank You for Your healing truth.***
***Help me to keep it in my heart.***

# BLESSED TO RECEIVE

*"Your kingdom come, Your will be done,*
*on earth as it is in heaven."*
MATTHEW 6:10 NIV

We humans were clearly designed to help one another in times of need. Whether it's opening a door for someone, changing a tire, or giving a pep talk, it sure feels good to be on the giving end when the opportunity presents itself. Don't you love it when you're being used by God to brighten someone else's day? Well, what if the tables are turned and you are the receiver? That's another story. For some of us, receiving help can be tough. We may like to appear strong and in control, or maybe we don't want to feel like we owe other people for anything. Receiving from others can be humbling. . .but it can be holy too. When we walk through difficult times, we may be blessed with people who come alongside us, wanting to help smooth our path a little. It could be by them making us meals, helping around the house, or by just sitting and listening to us as we pour out our hearts on a rough day. No matter what, it's good to remember that this is one wonderful way God provides for us on our toughest journeys. Those moments we've spent on our knees asking for His presence, those prayers that others have lifted up for our comfort—those things are answered in many ways, and one of them is with the hands and feet and hearts of those who care.

Here's a good thing to remember when someone reaches out: it blesses others to bless you. If you are able to receive another person's goodness with grace, you can always remember that down the road you'll have the chance to do the same for someone else. And this is how the Kingdom comes among us, bringing comfort, peace, and love—one willing soul at a time.

***Lord, help me to receive all You have for me. When others reach out, may I graciously accept the help they so generously give.***

"WHAT WE HAVE
ONCE ENJOYED
WE CAN
NEVER LOSE.
ALL THAT WE LOVE
DEEPLY BECOMES
A PART OF US."

HELEN KELLER

# BRIGHT SPOTS

*Weeping may endure for a night,*
*but joy comes in the morning.*
*PSALM 30:5 NKJV*

There's something about the sunrise that lifts our spirits. When we imagine God speaking His glorious creation into existence, we can't help but see how He made morning to give us all a fresh start. Nighttime is notorious for being a struggle during the difficult seasons of our lives. But when the light of day breaks through, it can give us a sense of hope again. On those long nights, we need to know the sun is on its way—that we're being given a new day, a new chance to live this life God has blessed us with. Anticipation like that is so important, but often, when we're on the journey of grief, we forget how much we need it. Days can seem long; nights can seem endless; it can seem like forever since we've felt a true sense of happiness.

There is something we can do for ourselves in our time of waiting that lifts our hearts, even just a little, and reminds us that brighter days are coming. We can give ourselves something to look forward to each day. It doesn't have to be big—just something we enjoy, something that makes us feel blessed and even reminds us of God's love for us. We might schedule a walk with a friend, some pampering at a local spa, or eating out at a favorite restaurant. Sure, right now these things might not bring the happiness we're used to, but they can at least serve to get us out of our little worlds and lift us up, even for a few moments. Scripture is filled with anticipation—the greatest hope being the hope of a Messiah who would rescue God's people from a world living in darkness. That Messiah—Jesus—is the reason we can look forward with hope, no matter what we're going through today. Try sitting down with your calendar and asking Him how you might add some bright spots to this season of life. He knows exactly what your heart needs each day.

*Lord, help me to see the hope*
*You bring with each new day.*
*You are the light of the world!*

# ANGER AND PEACE

*My dear brothers and sisters, take note of this:*
*Everyone should be quick to listen,*
*slow to speak and slow to become angry.*
*JAMES 1:19 NIV*

When it comes to feelings, a lot of us would rather keep our anger well hidden. We're told that acting upset is not a good thing and that people would rather hear us praising than complaining about something or someone. Anger gives us an edge, and aren't we supposed to be walking around with love and peace in our hearts? Times of grief can easily bring up anger in our lives. We may have unfinished business with our loved one or discord in our family; we may find ourselves frustrated that no one seems to understand us; we may even be mad at God, wondering why He would allow us the experience of loss. Whatever it is that settles in our hearts, it doesn't feel right, but we may not believe we have the strength to deal with it. But God knew we would experience angry emotions—that's why He gave us plenty of reminders in His Word to turn us back toward peace. As the apostle Paul shared: "Don't sin by letting anger control you. Don't let the sun go down while you are still angry" (Ephesians 4:26 NLT). We need to give ourselves grace on this journey, though—after all, God does!

If anger is a struggle for you, consider setting aside some time to pray about its source. Where is it coming from? How long has it been there? What would you tell Jesus about it if He were sitting right there with you? Giving emotions a voice can bring a sense of calm to your heart. Knowing you are speaking to the One who already understands every detail about you and loves you anyway should help you move further down the path to peace. Reaching out to a friend or mentor can help ease the burden too. It's good to remember that God often works through people to show us His extravagant love and grace. It may not all happen at once, but you can trust that He is healing you in His time, in His way. However you are released from your burden, may your load be lightened and may you know how deeply He cares.

*Lord, please reveal any anger in me,*
*and help me to live in Your peace.*

# HIS EYES

***Keep me as the apple of your eye;***
***hide me in the shadow of your wings.***
*PSALM 17:8 ESV*

Here's a life-giving prayer we can pray anytime we need encouragement: *Lord, help me to see myself through Your eyes.* Think about the way you look at someone you love—someone you cherish with all of your heart. Now imagine your heavenly Father, whose love is infinitely greater than that, looking at *you*. Just think, when He sees you, He sees someone He spoke into existence. Because He had the *idea* of you, He surely delights in beholding His beautiful creation: "Oh yes," Psalm 139:13–14 declares, "You shaped me first inside, then out; You formed me in my mother's womb. I thank You, High God—You're breathtaking! Body and soul, I am marvelously made!" (THE MESSAGE).

He also looks at you with compassion. He has seen every tear and heard every silent prayer of your heart in your loss. He knows what it is to be wrapped in human skin and to grieve. He deeply understands your struggle: "As a father shows compassion to his children, so the LORD shows compassion to those who fear him" (Psalm

103:13 ESV). He looks at you through eyes of patience. You may expect a lot of yourself, or you may wonder why you aren't in the place you feel like you should be. But He knows exactly where you are on this journey and why, and He is bringing about redemption in your life: "He has made everything beautiful in its time" (Ecclesiastes 3:11 NIV).

And finally, He looks at you with hope. He knows there is deep joy being birthed beneath your brokenheartedness. He is using every little bit of your life for your good, and He sees who you are becoming in the midst of even your most difficult days. Romans 8:28 reminds us: "That's why we can be so sure that every detail in our lives of love for God is worked into something good" (THE MESSAGE). The next time you feel invisible or defeated, think about your Father's loving gaze. He was with you from the moment you were created, and He will be with you all the days of your life.

*Lord, thank You for creating me!*
*Help me to see myself the way*
*that You see me today.*

# LIVING HIS LOVE

***For we are his workmanship,***
***created in Christ Jesus for good works,***
***which God prepared beforehand,***
***that we should walk in them.***

*EPHESIANS 2:10 ESV*

Moving through a time of grief can bring a lot of change, and it's possible that the things we're usually interested in—our hobbies or our goals—will not have the pull they once did. It's not that these things will forever be out of our lives; it's just that we need a break. We may seek more quiet time, more prayer time, or more down time—whatever that looks like for us. It can be easy to slip off the radar and stay hidden from the world. We all need that God-given time, and there's nothing wrong with taking a break. But sometimes it's helpful to find little ways to encourage ourselves to make connections again. One thing we can do is remember why we are here on Earth: to follow Jesus by living out His love for the world. Every day we are blessed to wake up is an opportunity to do that. Blessing someone in His Name brings joy to our hearts because that's what we were designed for.

This may be a strange time for you, but it can also be a time when you ask the Lord how you might bless someone in your life. It could be the smallest thing, but it is sure to bless your heart as much as it does theirs. You may even make it a daily practice to ask, *Lord, how can I share Your love with someone today?* Our heavenly Father is never short on ideas. He knows that you are walking through a difficult time, and He is surely happy to provide a way for you to experience His joy, even for a few moments a day. Write a letter, make a phone call, visit someone who is lonely. Many people find it helps to take their minds off themselves for a bit, to intentionally take a break from the sadness that's been so present and familiar. If you choose to take a step in that direction, God will surely meet you there.

***Lord, how might I bless someone today?***
***Help me to live out Your love for the world.***

# HIS SHALOM

*"I have told you all this*
*so that you may have peace in Me.*
*Here on earth you will have*
*many trials and sorrows. But take heart,*
*because I have overcome the world."*

*JOHN 16:33 NLT*

In the most tumultuous times of our lives, it is a wonderful thing to remember that peace is a Person. From the beginning of time, God has blessed His beloved people with the peace of His presence. Right now we may find ourselves praying for peace often—for a sense of "okay-ness" amid our circumstances, for quiet in our hearts, for acceptance of whatever He brings into our lives. Let us always remember that long before peace was something we could feel, it existed as part of our Maker. "For He Himself is our peace," Paul reminded Jesus's followers in Ephesians 2:14 (NIV). While the "feeling" of peace may come and go for us, the God of peace never leaves our side.

The Bible uses the Hebrew word *shalom* for peace, describing a sense of wholeness or completeness. It is our loving Father's desire that we experience that *shalom* in Him, and He draws us to Himself in countless ways in order to give us that gift, especially in the midst of our struggles. Our job is simply to receive. No matter what kind of day we're having, how "holy" we feel, or how discouraged we've been, we are offered a new start in His presence.

Consider taking a moment, finding a comfy spot, and opening your hands as a sign of all you are receiving from Him. Remember: the world will offer countless ways to bring that sense of peace, but only One stands ready in any moment to give the blessing of *shalom*. In John 14:27, Jesus comforted His followers who were not ready to let go of Him in the flesh: "I am leaving you with a gift—peace of mind and heart. And the peace I give is a gift the world cannot give. So don't be troubled or afraid" (NLT). This gift is ours in Him, and the more we can remind ourselves of His closeness with us, the more deeply we will feel it in our days.

***Lord, remind me often of Your*** **shalom.**
***I receive all You have for me today.***

# LETTING GO

***Let your eyes look straight ahead;***
***fix your gaze directly before you.***
***Give careful thought to the paths for your***
***feet and be steadfast in all your ways.***

*PROVERBS 4:25–27 NIV*

There's something big God has asked us to leave in His hands. It's something we often try to hold on to or wish we could change—something that can weigh us down with a load we were never meant to carry. What is it? *Our past*. When we're living through a season of loss, it can be extra tough to trust that God has covered those days gone by with His love. We might be dealing with regrets—those would-have, should-have thoughts that bring us down and keep us stuck. Guilt may sneak in and cause us to be hard on ourselves. We may forget God's grace and focus on what we perceive as our shortcomings, and all the while, He looks on us with compassion, wanting to remove that weight and bless us with His peace.

Throughout His Word, God rescues His people from the mistakes of their past and invites them to look toward a hope-filled future with Him: "Forget the former things; do not dwell on the past. See, I am doing a new thing! Now it springs up; do you not perceive it? I am making a way in the wilderness and streams in the wasteland (Isaiah 43:18–19 NIV). We can trust that He is always working to lighten our load and help us find freedom from anything the enemy would use to keep us down. If there are things we wish we'd done differently, we can bring them to Him, ask His forgiveness, and let them go. Even if we have to do it more than once to convince ourselves, He has promised to hear, to forgive, and to remove those things as far from us as the east is from the west. First John 1:9 reminds us: "If we confess our sins, he is faithful and just to forgive us our sins and to cleanse us from all unrighteousness" (ESV). Our God is *for* us. . .yesterday, today, and forever. He stands ready to free us from whatever we're carrying in life.

***Lord, thank You for holding my past, present, and future in Your hands.***

# MOUNTAINS AND VALLEYS

*I will give thanks to You,*
*Lord, with all my heart;*
*I will tell of all Your wonderful deeds.*
*PSALM 9:1 NIV*

We've all had mountaintop experiences in our life journeys, and, given the choice, most of us would surely have stayed there as long as we could. We may have enjoyed a sense of happiness and contentment, peace, and freedom from stress—maybe even a strong awareness of God's presence and purpose for our lives. And then come the valleys—the everyday grind, the difficulties we'd rather not face, the times when we may even question God's goodness in the midst of a storm. There may not be a lot we can do to change those circumstances, but we can choose what we will focus on as we experience them.

One of the most encouraging things we can do for ourselves is to remember that the same God who has allowed us to walk through this difficult time is the One who has provided those seasons of joy in the past. And not only that, but He will bring us out of this valley and into beautiful places in our lives again if we just trust His faithfulness.

Here is more good news: as we walk through the low places with Jesus, He plants the seeds of joy and gratitude in our hearts. We may not feel like singing out in praise, but if we invite Him to do His loving work in us, we will notice simple reasons to smile and be thankful along the way. No matter how deep the valleys have been, He provides little mountaintops in the midst of them that lift our hearts, even just for a moment. He can make the everyday sacred, reminding us that nothing is beyond His reach, that anything can be transformed by His loving touch. From the beginning of time, God's people have been called to remember His faithfulness, and we can do the same. Ask Jesus to remind you of those times you've been blessed, and trust that He has more in store for you than you can imagine. May you sense His goodness each day, and store up more and more of His blessings in your heart.

***Lord, remind me of the good You've brought into my life, and help me to see more of it each day.***

# FIRST THOUGHTS

***You go before me and follow me.***
***You place Your hand of blessing on my head.***
*PSALM 139:5 NLT*

When we walk into a new day, it's a wonderful thing to remember that Someone has gone before us to blaze the trail. Our God is the Way Maker and the Navigator, the One who allows our lives to unfold before us, and the One who gently guides us through. From the moment we wake up, we can depend on His presence, knowing that it is His desire and delight to walk with us. It's so easy to become caught up in our to-dos or focused on our fears and frustrations and miss those moments with Him. This can set us up for a day that's filled with more anxiety and less peace, more discouragement and less hope. God has given us powerful minds, and it's important to remember that we get to choose our thoughts, which will flow out into our feelings and actions throughout the day.

As II Corinthians 10:5 reminds us: "We take captive every thought to make it obedient to Christ" (NIV). When we go through tough times, this is vital. We need to recognize the discouraging words of the enemy each morning so that we can shut them out and listen for God's encouragement over everything else. And even when we feel stuck or aren't sure which way to go, we can rest assured that He is just a prayer away. He reminds us that when the journey feels impossible or confusing, we should hold on to Him with all we have: "Trust in the Lord with all your heart and lean not on your own understanding; in all your ways submit to Him, and He will make your paths straight (Proverbs 3:5–6 NIV). When you wake up, remember that You have a constant Companion who is ready to lead you down those paths, to walk beside you, and to carry you through any rough spots you may face.

*Lord, may I walk through every day with You.*
*Thank You for being my best friend.*

# STEP BY STEP

*Cast all your anxiety on Him*
*because He cares for you.*
*1 PETER 5:7 NIV*

Picture two tall ladders—one has rungs that are very close to each other, and you don't have to strain yourself to climb it. The other's rungs are far apart, and your legs can barely reach each one. If we're not in a hurry, most of us would choose the first; it may take a while, but those small steps will get us to the top in the end. Sometimes on the journey of grief, we just want to rise above it all as fast as possible and in as few steps as possible. We opt for that second ladder, even with its rungs impossibly spread out; we want it to take us to the top quickly.

Our prayers for healing may not be for small steps; we may be asking God for miracles today—to take the pain away, to free us from the burden we carry, to help us feel like ourselves again. We may be doing whatever we can—reaching out for connection with others, seeking some form of therapy, reminding ourselves of God's promises to show up for us. And while we pray for great progress, we can feel discouraged when things don't happen as we hoped they would. We might imagine God gently reminding us that we are moving up that ladder in little ways every day. While we wish for instant relief, we may instead find small comforts that add up. While we pray for great faith in the midst of the storm, we may discover that our doubt is slowly diminishing, and little bits of light are shining through. While we may feel down and discouraged at times, we may also be able to look back and see how, little by little, hope is finding its way into our hearts.

God can work in big ways, too, but often, it's about meeting Him in the moment, trusting that He's bringing us a little further along. And when we ask Jesus to walk with us, it isn't us climbing the ladder, anyway—it's Him, carrying us up, step by step. The more we are able to give everything over to Him, the more strength we will have on the journey, no matter how long it takes.

***Lord, remind me daily that You are providing all the healing I need, step by step.***

# YOUR PURPOSE

***For we are God's handiwork,***
***created in Christ Jesus to do good works,***
***which God prepared in advance for us to do.***
*EPHESIANS 2:10 NIV*

There may be times in our lives when we have a great sense of our purpose. We could be doing something we feel that God has called us to do, we may be reaching out to others with His love, or perhaps we've been moved to spend time in prayer for certain people who need Him. It's a wonderful feeling to sense His guidance and goodness in our days.

Times of grief can be different, though. We may struggle to find meaning in our moments; we may feel overtaken by sadness, spending our days in survival mode, just trying to put one foot in front of the other. It's the struggle of being human in a world that wasn't supposed to be broken. Our loving Father is here for us, though, and He has very specific ways to help us through. One of these ways is reminding us of our purpose. In Him, we are more than our grief; we are more than our struggle; our daily lives are filled with meaning, but we must learn to look and listen for it.

God gives us all the time and space we need to walk through these journeys of loss, but He wants us to know they're not meaningless. He still desires to use us—to pour His love through us, and to give us opportunities to help bring His beautiful Kingdom to Earth. This may look different than we're used to right now. We may wonder how we could possibly contribute anything in our current state. But He knows just how to awaken our hearts to our sense of worth. He reminds us that we are a precious and important part of His family, and we are called to be a part of all He's doing, even when we feel weak and insignificant.

Remember this on the rough days: your life matters infinitely to the One who created you. He is there to remind you each day of your purpose and to encourage you to keep walking with Him.

***Lord, please remind me of my purpose.***
***Help me to hear Your voice today.***

FROM THE END
OF THE EARTH
I WILL CRY TO YOU,
WHEN MY HEART
IS OVERWHELMED;
LEAD ME TO
THE ROCK THAT IS
HIGHER THAN I.

PSALM 61:2 NKJV

# YOUR STORY

***"Fear not, for I have redeemed you;
I have called you by your name;
You are Mine."***

*ISAIAH 43:1 NKJV*

Our Maker knew from the beginning, as He looked upon our fallen world, that we would need redemption. Not just some cleaning up and fixing up but a complete transformation—a total renewal of our stories, bringing our lives from darkness to light. People throughout history have longed for this to happen. Surely even those who had never heard of God recognized that something wasn't right, that something needed to change, but how? What a gift we have been given to live in a world where that Redeemer has come. We no longer have to wonder why things are so broken, or how goodness is going to come through, or when we will finally get to experience God's presence. In Christ, we have the answers. We have the gift of His Spirit here to lead us, and we know we will never walk alone.

However, these stories of ours. . . there's a lot to them. They just aren't like the *Once upon a times* in our favorite fairy tales. But the truth is, our stories are being redeemed just as God is renewing everything in all creation. When we trust Jesus with our lives, that story we've been living takes a radical turn on a new path. Everything we experience becomes a way of learning God's love for us. Every time of blessing becomes a chapter of praise. But every hard time finds us wishing that part wasn't written. Our toughest seasons remind us that even though an eternally loving Author is guiding our lives, He is helping us navigate through a broken world. We may not be able to make out the story ahead, but we can have complete trust that the One who leads us will provide all the peace and comfort we need as we draw close to Him. We can also trust that as hard as this time is, He will bring beauty from the ashes in ways we just can't imagine. Let us remember on our darkest days that He offers glimmers of hope if we will watch for them. And let us give thanks that the story He is writing with our lives has a glorious ending, no matter what we face along the way.

***Lord, my story is Yours. Help me to see all the ways You show up in it.***

# MAKING A WAY

***Jesus looked at them intently and said, "Humanly speaking, it is impossible. But with God everything is possible."***

*MATTHEW 19:26 NLT*

When we're going through tough times, there can be days that feel more encouraging—like we're moving forward, we're feeling more ups than downs, we have a sense of hope that carries us along. And then there are those days when we feel absolutely stuck. It seems like we've been feeling this way forever, and we wonder what we can possibly do to be free of whatever is holding us down. First, it's important to know that we're in good company. The Bible is full of people who were longing for things to change and wondering *when* and *how* and *if* it would ever happen. The good news is, these stories were told to remind us that there is a God who shows up in the midst of our discouragement and makes a way where there was no way. But it all happens in His time, which isn't our favorite thing to hear. We can trust, however, that no matter what we're feeling at the moment, He is at work beneath the surface to bring about our healing and to reveal Himself to us in new ways. Even if we feel discouraged, we can trust that He knows exactly what we need when we need it.

Imagine the story of Israel's Exodus: the Israelites are being pursued by Pharoah and his Egyptian army. As Moses leads them to flee through the wilderness, they cry out in despair, believing that their wandering will never end. But at just the right time, God shows up to make a way with the parting of the sea to rescue them from their enemies and bring them into a new place. When we feel stuck, we can trust that He is working to bring us into a new place too. It may happen little by little, or it may happen in a big way, but as long as we call on Him, it *will* happen. The psalmist reminds us: "Wait for the LORD; be strong and take heart and wait for the LORD" (Psalm 27:14 NIV). May these words encourage you today.

***Lord, remind me that***
***You are always at work.***
***Help me to trust Your timing***
***and to be encouraged today.***

# HIS CHILD

***Jesus said, "Let the little children come to Me, and do not hinder them, for the kingdom of heaven belongs to such as these."***

*MATTHEW 19:14 NIV*

Through the years, many artists have imagined this scene between Jesus and the children He cherished. They have pictured joy in His eyes, little ones climbing on His knees and resting in His arms, scenes full of the tangible love of our Father God, brought to Earth by the Son. Children are the picture of humility and helplessness—they are little bundles of need, constantly reaching out to their protectors. As we grow out of childhood, we begin to expect so much of ourselves, and we lose that sense of simple dependence on the ones who love us most.

When was the last time you saw yourself as one of God's little ones, approaching Him with absolutely nothing to offer but your presence, just wanting to know how much He cherishes you? When we're grieving, that's exactly how we can feel sometimes—empty and desperate, needing to know just how near He is. These are the precious times when we can call out for our

"Abba" and trust that He sees us through those beautiful, all-knowing, fatherly eyes. We can sense that special kind of love poured out toward us as His little children, and our hearts can respond with simple gratitude—just an overwhelming sense of being enough because we belong to *Him*. We don't have to find words; we don't have to feel holy; we don't even have to know why we're coming to Him. We can simply rest in the truth that our Father surrounds us with His pure love, just as we are as His beloved creations, needing His presence more than anything else on Earth. He delights in our dependence, just as any loving father is blessed in knowing he is needed by his child. What a gift to know His arms are forever open. May you sense His presence today.

***Lord, help me to see myself***
***as Your precious child. May I rest in***
***Your loving presence today.***

# THE GREAT EXCHANGE

*Then Jesus said, "Come to Me,*
*all of you who are weary*
*and carry heavy burdens,*
*and I will give you rest."*
MATTHEW 11:28 NLT

This is one of the most comforting invitations of Jesus: we bring to Him all that weighs us down, and He promises to relieve us. What a gift! But just like all of His words to us, we need to keep these extra close, especially during our most difficult seasons. It isn't hard to tell whether we're finding our rest in Him, or whether we're starting to operate in our own strength. Consider asking yourself these three questions: *Am I feeling hopeless and discouraged?* Are you in survival mode—going through the motions, seeing everything through a dark lens? *Am I worn out from being on an emotional roller coaster?* Are you exhausted from all the ups and downs you've been feeling? *Do I just want people to leave me alone?* Would you rather avoid having to interact with others right now, preferring to be by yourself? These are things we can all struggle with in times of loss, but Jesus reminds us that He's here to share the burden. We can bring all our feelings, our weariness, and our isolation to Him, and He will gently guide us back onto the path of peace and assurance. Sure, it will happen in His time and in His way, but we can hold fast to His promise that He will help us through.

"Take My yoke upon you and learn from Me," He reminds us, "for I am gentle and humble in heart, and you will find rest for your souls. For My yoke is easy, and My burden is light" (Matthew 11:29–30 NIV). It's a beautiful exchange. He has something for us to carry, but it looks nothing like the pain we're laying down. And it's something we carry along with Him—His love for the world. The more of our burdens we are able to bring to Him, the more of that love we can share. Just remember, His grace is limitless, and He gives us all the time we need to come to Him and lay it all down.

***Lord, thank You for sharing my burdens. May my heart be open to more of Your love.***

# IN HIM

*This means that anyone who belongs*
*to Christ has become a new person.*
*The old life is gone; a new life has begun!*
*II CORINTHIANS 5:17 NLT*

There's no doubt that grief changes us. When we lose someone who was a special part of our lives, we can feel like a part of us is missing, and nothing prepares us for that feeling. We may even see ourselves differently without that person connected with us here on Earth. Things will shift; perspectives might change; our daily lives could be rearranged without the one we love. All of this can leave us feeling unsettled and even a bit lost as we try to move forward with each day. This can be a wonderful time to be reminded of who we are in Christ—and that no matter what changes, how much we have to let go, or how we feel about ourselves, our identity in Him remains secure. If you find yourself feeling insecure or uncertain, remember these important truths:

- *You are a precious child of God*: "But to all who believed Him and accepted Him, He gave the right to become children of God" (John 1:12 NLT).
- *You were created for a purpose*: "For we are God's

masterpiece. He has created us anew in Christ Jesus, so we can do the good things He planned for us long ago" (Ephesians 2:10 NLT).

- *You are one in spirit with God*: "But the person who is joined to the Lord is one spirit with Him" (I Corinthians 6:17 NLT).
- *You are never alone*: "All of you together are Christ's body, and each of you is a part of it" (I Corinthians 12:27 NLT).
- *You have victory over the enemy*: "For the LORD your God is going with you! He will fight for you against your enemies, and He will give you victory!" (Deuteronomy 20:4 NLT).
- *You have God's strength within you*: "For I can do everything through Christ, who gives me strength" (Philippians 4:13 NLT).
- *The peace of God is yours*: "For Christ Himself has brought peace to us" (Ephesians 2:14 NLT).

These are just a few of the beautiful gifts that are ours in Christ. May you be reminded each day of who you are in Him.

***Lord, what a gift to know that my true identity is found in You. Help me to rest in that truth today.***

# STANDING FIRM

***For no one can lay a foundation other than that which is laid, which is Jesus Christ.***

*I CORINTHIANS 3:11 ESV*

There are some days when it feels like our feet have been pulled out from under us. We don't know which end is up, and we try desperately to find something to hold on to. When we find ourselves feeling lost like that, we can head quickly down a path of anxiety that steals any moments of peace and joy we hoped to have. This journey of grief is unpredictable, and we need to know there can be days that will throw us for a loop. We may have no idea why we woke up feeling the way we did, or why it's harder to get our bearings, or why we can't seem to find our way out of this rough spot. But one thing is absolutely certain: *no matter how we feel at the moment, we have a firm foundation in Jesus Christ, and He will never move*. We have a place in our hearts to return to again, and again—a place to hold on to in the midst of what feels like chaos.

As Jesus reminds us in His Word: "Everyone then who hears these words of mine and does them will be like a wise man who built his house on the rock. And the rain fell, and the floods came, and the winds blew and beat on that house, but it did not fall, because it had been founded on the rock" (Matthew 7:24–25 ESV). The enemy may try and convince us that we are standing on shaky ground, but we need to remind him that we have found refuge in the immovable One. It's a life-giving image to have on days when it feels like there is a lot happening that's out of our control. The One who is in control has given us Himself to return to, to hold fast to, to stand strong on. As we keep our eyes on Him, everything else will fall into place.

***Lord, help me to hold on to You when I feel lost.<br>I know that You are always there for me.***

# NO COMPARISON

*The Lord will fulfill his purpose for me;*
*your steadfast love, O Lord, endures forever.*
*PSALM 138:8 ESV*

Do you ever struggle with comparing yourself to others? It seems to be all too common these days as we are flooded with social media snapshots and all sorts of storytelling devices. It's hard enough on our good days, but what about during the tough times? We're doing all we can to keep it together while the people around us may seem blissfully unaware that all is NOT right with the world. We may be dealing with loneliness, sadness, and hurt and, if we're honest, the last thing we want is to run across people who seem to be thriving and having the time of their lives. It's not that we can't be happy for them at some point; it's just that right now, we have all we can handle. It can be easy for envy to creep in, or discouragement, as we wonder when we'll finally feel like we're on the bright side again. Here are three important things we can remember if we find ourselves struggling:

1. Whether it's a real-life interaction or a few moments

on a screen, we're witnessing a small part of a person's world when we see them. If they aren't having a hard time right now, we can be sure they've had their share. Whether it was yesterday, or something they will experience tomorrow, we all walk through difficult seasons—it's something that connects us as human beings living in a broken world.

2. We always have a choice about how to respond to people. If we catch ourselves wishing to be in their shoes, or if we find ourselves feeling down as a result of comparison, we can always lift our hearts in a simple prayer: *Lord, thank You for my life. Please bless this person in every way.*

3. Remember, God is working in our lives just as much as He is in theirs. While we're in a challenging season, His promises to lead us through are true and eternal. And just as with all His children, He desires for us to experience His joy and His peace in this life, and He knows exactly how that's going to happen as we continue to trust in Him.

***Lord, thank You for my life. I know You have goodness in store for me.***

# HEAVENLY NOTES

*Sing and make music*
*from your heart to the Lord.*
*EPHESIANS 5:19 NIV*

What kind of music speaks to your heart? Is it the strum of a guitar, the clear notes of a piano, an angelic voice singing out in praise—or maybe something totally different? God's gift of music speaks to each of us uniquely, bringing a smile to our faces or a tear to our eyes seemingly out of nowhere; it can stir us deeply.

There are times in our lives when words just don't feel like enough—whether they are the comforting words of others or the things we speak to ourselves as we're just trying to make it through another day. King David knew this feeling three thousand years ago, and he's an example of someone who reached beyond words to bring God's comfort and peace through music. He knew there was a depth to be found in the melodies he created, and his worship through sound brought him into God's presence in new ways. The Psalms are wonderful examples of a heart crying out to God, drawing close to Him in praise and lamentation. We can only imagine the music that accompanied that poetry as David sang it out for all to hear. It's something for us to keep in mind, all these centuries later, when life brings the hardest things for us to face. Music is a heavenly gift, and it may just be what God provides in some of our toughest moments. Whether it's the praise songs at church, a song shared by a friend, or our own ability to pick up an instrument and play a favorite tune, it's good to keep our ears and our hearts open to that special way God may be speaking. Music is a beautiful love language, and it's one way that God may be drawing us to Himself in comfort and in care.

*Lord, help me to be aware*
*of Your gift of music.*
*Thank You for such a beautiful way*
*to connect with You.*

# ENCOURAGE ONE ANOTHER

*Jesus spoke to the people once more and said, "I am the light of the world. If you follow Me, you won't have to walk in darkness, because you will have the light that leads to life."*
*JOHN 8:12 NLT*

God never wastes our difficult journeys. One thing we can always count on is that He will bring light from the dark: "For it is you who light my lamp; the Lord my God lightens my darkness" (Psalm 18:28 ESV). He's been doing it since the creation of the world. It may take a while for us to see, but as we look to Him in our struggles, He works in our hearts to help us find hope and purpose again. And it may be hard to imagine right now, but one way that happens is when He gives us the opportunity down the road to encourage others who are going through the same thing. Loss is something we all experience in our own time, and if we are open to His leading, He may guide us to someone who needs to know they can make it through too.

You may have been on the receiving end of someone's

encouragement—someone who knows what it's like to grieve and experience God's healing. His Word reminds us that "two are better than one" (Ecclesiastes 4:9 NIV) and to "encourage one another and build each other up" (1 Thessalonians 5:11 NIV). There may even be others in your life who are going through hard times right now. Consider reaching out. Connecting with one another can help bring comfort and hope to both of your hearts. Then, in God's time, you can pass those things along to someone else who needs it. Many ministries have been born out of peoples' struggles. Consider the apostle Paul, who suffered much in this life but clung to hope through it all. "For I consider that the sufferings of this present time are not worth comparing with the glory that is to be revealed to us" (Romans 8:18 ESV). Just remember, you will get through this time, and if you keep looking to God for your purpose, He will bring goodness out of your most difficult experience. You are precious to Him, and not a moment of your life will be wasted.

***Lord, thank You for Your light in the darkness. Help me to look to You for my purpose each day.***

# DEAR YOU

***He will cover you with His feathers.***
***He will shelter you with His wings.***
***PSALM 91:4 NLT***

Some of us were blessed to grow up with loving parents who cared for us and protected us, who were there for us through the toughest times in our lives. Others may have had a mentor or another adult who adopted them and showed them that parental love. Still others may not have had that gift in their lives. Regardless, every one of us has a gracious heavenly Father who desires to pour out His love on us in so many ways. In Paul's letters in the New Testament, God is described as "Father" over forty times. And not only did Jesus address God as "Abba" (an intimate word for Father), but He taught His disciples to do the same. God's desire to love us as family is clear, whether or not we have known this kind of love on Earth. When we lose someone close to us, His Father's heart reaches out to shelter us with comfort and care. He knows what it is to experience loss, and He wants us to come to Him so that He can walk us through. Sometimes it's hard to feel that comfort as we wrestle with our feelings and fight discouragement and despair.

Here's something you might want to try so you can become more aware of His presence on the journey. You can use a prayer journal or just a blank sheet of paper and a pen. It takes some quiet reflection and a simple turning of your heart and mind toward Him. Write a letter to yourself, imagining what your heavenly Father might be saying to you. It may be based on the love your earthly father gave you, or it may just be whatever comes to your mind when you envision such a love being shared. Think of Scripture—of all God's promises to care for you through the most difficult times. How would His comfort come through to you? What might He want to say to draw you closer to Him? Keep your note as a reminder that you are never alone—that you are loved beyond imagining. Thank Him for all the ways He shows up for you to see you through.

***Lord, what do You have to say***
***to me as my loving Father?***
***Help me to find comfort in all Your promises.***

BLESSED
ARE THOSE
WHO MOURN,
FOR THEY
WILL BE
COMFORTED.

MATTHEW 5:4 NIV

# SO BLESSED

***From His abundance we have all received one gracious blessing after another.***

*JOHN 1:16 NLT*

There's something spirit-lifting we can do during those times when our hearts feel heavy. It may not be the first thing we think of, but it's something that can bring us joy in the moment and help give us a fresh outlook. You've probably heard of it a few times, and maybe even made it a regular practice. What is it? *Count your blessings*. It's such a simple thing—three words people may throw around a lot, but when we truly apply them, they can make a big difference. On tough days, it's easy to take on a doubtful outlook as we notice the ways we feel like God hasn't shown up or focus on something we wish was different. These things can pull us down quickly, taking our eyes off the good and true and turning our minds toward the negative. But if we remind ourselves often to lift our hearts, we can find ourselves giving thanks rather than regretting or sinking into sadness.

When things start to weigh you down, remember: "Every good gift and every perfect gift is from above, coming down from the Father of lights, with whom there is no variation or shadow due to change" (James 1:17 ESV). Even in our most challenging seasons, He is there, showering us with goodness in His own way. Sometimes it takes some reflection on the big picture to see how God has worked on our behalf; sometimes, it's there in the details of our days—so small we might have missed it if we hadn't been looking closely. Taking those few moments to name our blessings draws us closer to Him, the lifter of our heads. The more we do, the more we will recognize the ways God shows up in our lives when we need Him most.

*Lord, remind me often to count my blessings.*
*Thank You for every good gift that You give.*

# NEVER ALONE

***You are the LORD, you alone.***
***You have made heaven, the heaven of heavens,***
***with all their host, the earth and all that is on it,***
***the seas and all that is in them;***
***and you preserve all of them;***
***and the host of heaven worships you.***
*NEHEMIAH 9:6 ESV*

Are there times when you have felt alone on this journey? Maybe even now—disconnected from friends, away from social media, or just choosing to bow out of public places? Our times of loneliness come and go, but we all know how it feels to be on our own, wishing for some connection. . .and not sure how to make it happen. Whenever we have that feeling, may we be reminded to look beyond our earthly experiences. We may not be able to see into the spiritual realm, but God assures us that we are never alone. Regardless of how much contact we have with human beings at the moment, His heavenly messengers are never far from us: "Are they not all ministering spirits sent out to serve for the sake of those who are to inherit salvation?" (Hebrews 1:14 ESV).

If we could see beyond our senses, what a battle we would witness, with the blessed assurance that our all-powerful God and His mighty angels will be victorious over all. We would realize that we never have to fear: "For he will command his angels concerning you to guard you in all your ways" (Psalm 91:11 ESV). Our hearts would be lifted by the worship that they continually offer: "Praise him, all his angels; praise him, all his hosts!" (Psalm 148:2 ESV). Yes, even in our alone time, we are forever in good company.

Consider using a few moments of your holy imagination to picture the beautiful scene around you. God, who knows exactly what you need right now, is not withholding anything as He carries you through this time and works within you for your healing. Every ministering spirit, every heavenly force of restoration, has been sent from your gracious Father to surround and encourage you. If loneliness ever creeps in, consider those things you can't see with your eyes, and let your heart be lifted with the knowledge that you are right in the center of your Father's love.

***Lord, remind me often that I'm never alone.***
***Thank You for all of Your heavenly messengers.***

# IN HIS HANDS

*We can make our plans,*
*but the Lord determines our steps.*
*PROVERBS 16:9 NLT*

There's something we all struggle with from time to time—especially in seasons of loss. And when we look back through the Bible, we see many of those who have gone before us wrestling with the same thing: *admitting we aren't in control*. When things seem to be going our way—when relationships are running smoothly, when jobs are successful, when prayers are answered in the way we're hoping—it's easy to feel more like we're running the show. We may appreciate God's presence in our lives, but we wouldn't call ourselves desperate for Him every day. Then, the toughest times come. The rug is pulled out from under us, and we may wonder why we're having to go through this, *how* we're going to get through it, and whether God is really there like He has promised. We may experience a sense of helplessness or hopelessness with the sudden realization that the whole situation is out of our hands. This is when He calls us to trust Him beyond our feelings—to admit that He knows every detail of our lives and the lives of our loved ones.

"Are not two sparrows sold for a penny?" Jesus reminded His disciples. "Yet not one of them will fall to the ground outside your Father's care. And even the very hairs of your head are all numbered. So don't be afraid; you are worth more than many sparrows" (Matthew 10:29–31 NIV). Nothing comes to us that doesn't pass through the loving hands of our Father first. The more we see ourselves and those we love as part of His story, the more we can relax our need to control our lives. He knows how hard this is for us, and He has filled His Word with gracious reminders to trust Him through the darkest, most confusing times. We can see how He has cared for His followers throughout history, and know that He is caring for us too. "O my people, trust in Him at all times. Pour out your heart to Him, for God is our refuge" (Psalm 62:8 NLT). May your heart rest in Him today.

***Lord, help me to release my need to control. I want to trust in You.***

# TAKE COURAGE

***"When you go through deep waters, I will be with you. When you go through rivers of difficulty, you will not drown. When you walk through the fire of oppression, you will not be burned up; the flames will not consume you."***

*ISAIAH 43:2 NLT*

You may be familiar with the Old Testament story of Shadrach, Meshach, and Abednego, three Israelite men who were thrown into a fiery furnace by Nebuchadnezzar II, King of Babylon. They were being punished for refusing to deny God and bow to the king's image. The men displayed great courage as they stood for what they believed, but they made it clear that they were relying on God alone to see them through. They answered the king's threat: "O Nebuchadnezzar, we do not need to defend ourselves before you. If we are thrown into the blazing furnace, the God whom we serve is able to save us. He will rescue us from your power, Your Majesty. But even if He doesn't, we want to make it clear to you, Your Majesty, that we will never serve your gods or worship the gold statue you have set up" (Daniel 3:16–18 NLT).

The king followed through, and they were bound

and thrown into the flames, but something miraculous happened: they were not burned. In fact, the king observed that there was now a *fourth* man in the fire, and he looked like a god. He called them out of the furnace, crying, "Shadrach, Meshach, and Abednego, servants of the Most High God, come out! Come here!" (Daniel 3:26 NLT).

Through the years, some people have believed that the fourth man was Christ, before He came to Earth. Others believe it was an angel. Regardless, it's clear that God showed up just as they believed He would, but it surely took an unimaginable amount of faith to follow Him through what they did. Remember that as you experience this time in your life. Some days, it takes courage just to get out of bed. But this courage isn't something you have to muster up on your own. God has promised you His presence, and if you can receive that promise by faith, you can walk through anything. If you find yourself doubting, it's okay. He is greater than your doubt. Just bring whatever you have to Him, and He will meet you there.

***Lord, I trust You for the faith and the courage I need today.***

# OUR HOPE

*So we fix our eyes not on what is seen, but on what is unseen, since what is seen is temporary, but what is unseen is eternal.*
*II CORINTHIANS 4:18 NIV*

So much of this faith journey is about hoping for things we can't yet see. Do you ever get tired of that? Especially in challenging times, when we are desperate for something to hold on to, we're told to "keep on keepin' on" and to trust that good things are coming. We just don't know how or when. This was true for God's people over and over in Scripture. They were promised deliverance and redemption and transformation, but the path to those things was rarely what they expected. They were led along moment by moment, day by day, surely looking for every possible reason to believe amid the doubts and fears that tried to fill their human minds.

Can you imagine how confused and hopeless Jesus's followers felt on the day He died? And then, how gloriously filled with hope those He appeared to must have been after He rose? Many gave their lives for Him, trusting completely that heaven awaited them, never having seen it. Today, we have the great gift of knowing

He is risen, but unlike those followers, we are asked to believe in a Savior we can't touch. Sometimes our faith is strong, and we trust His presence beyond our senses. We have specific reasons for the hope in our hearts—undeniable ways God has shown up in our lives. Other times, life is heavy, and we can forget the ways He has been there for us. We just need to know He is real and He is right here with us. Jesus has always had a way of reaching the hopeless and discouraged among us. If you ever find yourself struggling, consider a simple prayer: *Jesus, fill me with hope*. He will never leave you alone in despair. It may not be when or how you're expecting, but He will find a way to lift your heart.

***Lord, You are my hope.***
***Please lift my heart each day to You.***

# TOTAL ECLIPSE

*"For I know the plans I have for you," says the Lord. "They are plans for good and not for evil, to give you a future and a hope."*

*JEREMIAH 29:11 TLB*

A total solar eclipse is one of those rare events that some folks will witness just once in their lifetime. Unlike a partial eclipse, a total eclipse happens when the moon passes in front of the sun long enough and completely enough to bring darkness to certain places on the earth. We twenty-first century humans are used to hearing about these events well in advance. There's plenty of news coverage and social media chatter as astronomers make their predictions about when an eclipse will take place. But imagine what it was like for ancient civilizations to be suddenly thrown into darkness in the middle of the day. This bright light in the sky that they planned their days around unexpectedly went dark; the thing they relied on to tell time, or to understand which direction they were headed, just disappeared. Of course, it only lasted for a few minutes, but they wouldn't have known that back then. They were probably quite confused, wondering what else they might look to if the light never returned.

When we experience loss in our lives, it can feel a bit like that sudden, unexpected darkness. The bright spots we've known in the past no longer give their light; our sources of happiness can feel empty and useless. Everything seems to cast a shadow as doubt and fear may begin to lurk in our hearts. It's helpful to remember that, just like the moon passing in front of the sun, this time isn't going to last forever. It may feel heavy and dark right now, but God is already moving to bring light back into our lives, even in small ways we may not see yet. This is a process, and He is walking with us through it all. Consider asking Him to show you ways He's bringing the light back. We can experience moments of hope and joy even in our grief, and when we do, let us remind ourselves that there is more to come. Our Creator has His ways, and the more we look to Him on this journey, the more assurance we'll have that there will be brighter days ahead.

***Lord, help me to remember that this season isn't forever. I believe that You are leading me through.***

# THE BREATH OF LIFE

*For the Spirit of God has made me,*
*and the breath of the Almighty gives me life.*
*JOB 33:4 NLT*

God's Word has much to say about breath, from the moment humankind was created—"Then the Lord God formed the man from the dust of the ground. He breathed the breath of life into the man's nostrils, and the man became a living person (Genesis 2:7 NLT)—to the moment Jesus gifted His followers with the Holy Spirit—"Again He said, 'Peace be with you. As the Father has sent Me, so I am sending you.' Then He breathed on them and said, 'Receive the Holy Spirit'" (John 20:21–22 NLT). Breath seems to represent the very Life of God, and it is clearly something we were created to need every moment. In times of tension, we might hold our breath; in times of stress, we might find ourselves breathing rapidly; in our most peaceful times, our breath comes in and out, slow and steady. Of course, we are so used to it, we don't even think about it most of the time. Thankfully, it's something our bodies just do.

When we go through difficult days and need to be reminded of God's peaceful presence, we can use our breath to center ourselves. It can be as simple as breathing in *1-2-3* and breathing out *1-2-3* while we imagine God's peace flowing though us. Or, we can try repeating a breath prayer like, *Breathe in God's goodness... Exhale His love.* Our compassionate Creator designed us in such a way that intentional breathing can calm both our bodies and our minds. And the most wonderful thing to remember in the tough times is that He is closer than our next breath. He is giving us the constant gift of life and asks only that we offer that life right back to Him. Next time you find yourself struggling and needing a sense of calm, take a moment to connect to that breath of life. Receive His peace and thank Him for His constant presence. He is nearer than you could ever imagine.

*Lord, thank You for the breath of life.*
*Help me to receive Your peace.*

# THE POWER OF STORY

*We will not hide these truths from our children;*
*we will tell the next generation*
*about the glorious deeds of the LORD,*
*about His power and His mighty wonders.*

*PSALM 78:4 NLT*

Storytelling has been around as long as creation. As far back as the book of Genesis, we see how people have told stories to preserve legacies, to warn each other about taking certain paths, and to encourage one another by illustrating what it looks like when we allow God to lead us. Stories inspire our imaginations and paint pictures that aren't created by facts alone. We want to hear how people felt, what kind of connections they made, and how they journeyed through even the hardest times. In our own seasons of grief, stories can be so powerful. We need to be reminded of all who have walked this path before us and made it through. Not only that, but we need those life-giving stories of people who looked to their loving Father to carry them and found peace and hope in His presence.

Especially in times when you feel discouraged, consider making connections with others who have trusted God to lead them through times of loss. Reach out to friends. Look up books or blogs that have been written by others in a similar journey. Be reminded again and again that you are not alone, or stuck, or lost. God has very specific ways He leads each of us through our times of need, and, just like all who look to Him, you will come out stronger on the other side. Our stories may look very different from the stories of other Jesus followers we come across, but we all have that wonderful common ground: we are all looking to Him to provide everything we need. And as God's Word reminds us, He may call us down the road to pass that comfort along to others who are struggling: "All praise to God, the Father of our Lord Jesus Christ. God is our merciful Father and the source of all comfort. He comforts us in all our troubles so that we can comfort others. When they are troubled, we will be able to give them the same comfort God has given us" (II Corinthians 1:3–4 NLT). Your story has a beautiful purpose, no matter what you face.

***Lord, help me to find encouragement through others who have followed You in their hardest times.***

# NEW THOUGHTS

***Be transformed by the renewal of your mind.***

*ROMANS 12:2 ESV*

As we walk through times of loss, our minds will naturally focus on all we're missing; we notice the place no longer filled by our loved one; we see the way we do life differently now without their presence. We have a sense of emptiness where fullness used to be, and we need time and space to adjust to this new way of being.

One thing we can do in the midst of these rough days is to ask God to renew our minds. We can pray for the ability to focus on all the blessings that were part of our lives because of the one we loved. We may even sit down with a notebook or journal and prayerfully consider writing a list of the gifts we have known through the life of the person we lost. Because we know that God has purpose for every life, we can ask Him to remind us of the many reasons we had this loving connection, and we can listen in the quiet of our hearts for His answers.

It's impossible to think about two things at once, so switching our minds to ways we've been blessed instead of thinking of all the things we're missing can be a gentle relief. We may even be reminded to give thanks for those gifts more often, bringing a deep sense of joy to our days. It may be a while before we feel happiness, but joy can bubble up beneath everything else—joy in knowing that we are part of the bigger picture of God's beautiful purpose; joy in trusting that He is guiding us through this season with soul-lifting love; joy that death and darkness do not have the last word in this story. Jesus, the light of life, is illuminating the way before us. Remember: "We have the mind of Christ [to be guided by His thoughts and purposes]" (I Corinthians 2:16 AMP). Consider asking Him to renew your mind today.

***Lord, bless me with good thoughts today. Remind me of the many gifts I've known through the life of my loved one.***

# GOD IS MOVING

*If God is for us, who can ever be against us?*
*Since He did not spare even His own Son*
*but gave Him up for us all,*
*won't He also give us everything else?*
ROMANS 8:31–32 NLT

Sometimes it's just good to be reminded that God is *for* us. He's not some neutral force in the sky or someone who's just here hanging out with us because He said He would. No, He's actively working on our behalf. He is bringing good into our lives. He is moving us forward from one spiritual destination to another. He is cheering us on like a parent attending their precious child's first game of the season. He wants the best for us, and He's arranging the details of our lives to create the most beautiful outcome possible. It's something to remember on our darkest days. His love is not just a thing that we've been given. It's an active force, healing what's broken, finding what's lost, lifting hearts that have been weighed down by the burdens of the world. And let us remember that He is *for* us, even on days when we aren't for ourselves—days when we feel weak, helpless, or less than worthy. That's when He loves us all the more.

Whenever you find yourself thinking discouraging thoughts or doubting that your life is moving forward in a positive direction, just remember how involved your heavenly Father is. Every thought, every belief, every action, every choice you make—it all matters to Him, and He's there with you working all things for your good. And not only is He cheering you on, but all who have ever known Him are watching and believing the best for you: "Therefore, since we are surrounded by such a huge crowd of witnesses to the life of faith, let us strip off every weight that slows us down, especially the sin that so easily trips us up. And let us run with endurance the race God has set before us" (Hebrews 12:1 NLT). May these reminders bring you confidence all your days.

***Lord, thank You for all the ways***
***Your love moves in my life.***
***I want to love You back with all my heart.***

THE LORD
IS CLOSE TO
THE BROKENHEARTED
AND SAVES THOSE
WHO ARE CRUSHED
IN SPIRIT.

PSALM 34:18 NIV

# GOD HUGS

*Starting from scratch,*
*He made the entire human race and made the earth hospitable, with plenty of time and space for living so we could seek after God, and not just grope around in the dark but actually find Him. He doesn't play hide-and-seek with us. He's not remote; He's near. We live and move in Him, can't get away from Him!*

ACTS 17:26–27 THE MESSAGE

We all need a hug once in a while. That gentle sense of reassurance from someone in our lives that we are connected with and cared for; that life may be tough, but love is bigger; that we may be struggling, but everything's going to be okay. Have you ever wished for a hug from God? The arms that hold the universe wrapped around you, offering unimaginable peace and reassurance that all will be well? Even though we don't have that tangible connection on this side of heaven, there is something we can do when we need those reminders that He's near—we can ask Him to show Himself to us in some way. Does that sound like too big of a thing to request? Have you ever considered it?

God's desire for us to seek Him is clear throughout

His Word. He *wants* our attention, *wants* us to long for His presence, *wants* us to invite Him into our lives. When we ask Him, *Lord, please show me Yourself today*, we are acknowledging His constant presence and inviting Him to show up in a special way that helps us to feel connected. It's like a hug from Him, and as our heavenly Father, He surely delights in providing those moments of revelation. They may not come right away or in a way that we expect, but we can trust that He will provide for us in His way, in His time. It may be through another person or through His creation; it may be what seems like a coincidence, or it could even be in a quiet moment of prayer. In our most difficult seasons, this is something we may find ourselves asking often. And do you know what? It's never too much for Him. Just as a caring parent stands ready to reassure a struggling child, so He stands ready to offer us the comfort of His love.

***Lord, please help me to see You in some way today. Thank You for all the ways You reveal Yourself to me.***

# OUR EVERYTHING

***And my God will supply every need of yours according to his riches in glory in Christ Jesus.***

***PHILIPPIANS 4:19 ESV***

Consider this: the way we experience the greatest struggles in our lives depends on the way we experience God. We are told that He is our everything, but it's for us to discover and live out what that truly means. If He really *is* all we need, then we can count on Him to show up in all the *ways* that we need. It's important to remember that His timing and His plan are always at work, so His provision may come in ways and at times when we least expect, but it will always come. God is described many ways in Scripture, but here are a few that may bring assurance in times of loss:

- *Jehovah Rapha*: The Lord our Healer — "He heals the brokenhearted and binds up their wounds" (Psalm 147:3 NIV). God draws us especially close in our sadness, all the while bringing healing to our hearts.
- *Jehovah Jireh*: The Lord our Provider — "So Abraham called the name of that place, 'The Lord will provide'; as it is said to this day, 'On the mount of the Lord it

shall be provided' (Genesis 22:14 ESV). He invites us to let go of worry and put our daily needs in His hands.

- *Jehovah Raah*: The Lord our Shepherd — "The LORD is my shepherd; I shall not want" (Psalm 23:1 ESV). He offers rest for our souls, anytime, anywhere.

- *El Roi*: The God Who sees me — "She gave this name to the LORD who spoke to her: 'You are the God who sees me'" (Genesis 16:13 NIV). He understands every part of us and loves us as we are.

- *Abba*: God, our true Father — "For you did not receive the spirit of slavery to fall back into fear, but you have received the Spirit of adoption as sons, by whom we cry, 'Abba! Father!'" (Romans 8:15 ESV). He calls us family.

Always remember, no matter how much we wrestle with doubt or despair, God will show up in the ways we need most. Hold on; be encouraged; trust His timing; know that you are cherished by Him, no matter what.

***Lord, You are my everything. Help me to turn to You and trust You every day.***

# OUR GENEROUS GOD

***You can be sure that God will take care of everything you need, His generosity exceeding even yours in the glory that pours from Jesus.***

*PHILIPPIANS 4:20 THE MESSAGE*

It's easy to take for granted all that we receive from God in a day. From the breath in our lungs to the loved ones in our lives to the spiritual encouragement we gain in times of struggle, our God is a generous God, and He delights in providing all that we need—and even more than we could ask for. There is a whole list of gifts that have come to us through Christ, and we can get so bogged down in life sometimes that we forget all that we have received because of Him. As Ephesians 1:3 reminds us, "Blessed be the God and Father of our Lord Jesus Christ, who has blessed us in Christ with every spiritual blessing in the heavenly places" (ESV).

In seasons of grief, we can feel closed off to these things. We want to feel better, but we can struggle with feeling bitter. We want to see God's goodness, but we may be wondering why He's allowed us to be in this place and how He's possibly going to bring us through this time. Let us remember that no matter how we feel on our end, He never stops giving on His end. He has so much to offer in a day, and we have the ability to choose whether to open our hearts to that, or to ignore those daily gifts and remain in the dark. Sometimes it's a challenge to lift our heads and acknowledge His gifts, but once we do, it sets us on a hopeful path—one where we can see Him at work in the details of our lives because we're looking for it.

To become more aware of His gifts, and to truly receive all He has for you, consider praying a simple prayer asking Him to open your mind and your heart to all He's blessing you with each day. Sometimes it can help to pray with your arms open in a posture of total surrender, recognizing that all you have comes from Him. However you choose to receive, just remember that you are His precious child and He loves to provide for all your needs—and then some!

***Lord, thank You for every gift You give.***
***May I receive all You have for me each day.***

# WRITTEN WORDS

***Draw near to God,***
***and he will draw near to you.***
*JAMES 4:8 ESV*

How do you feel about journaling? Some people feel it's a natural way to express themselves, and they have notebooks full of life collected through the years. Others feel intimidated about putting their thoughts into words and would rather keep them within, in the quiet of their hearts. Regardless of your experience with the written word, prayer journaling can be a powerful support during the most challenging times in our lives. Putting our hearts into words and offering them to a caring Father who is eager to listen and respond can be a healing thing. A journal can capture the rawness of feeling, the needs of a day, unexpected discoveries, and even the acknowledgement of blessings. We can collect encouraging bits of God's Word there to revisit when we need them most. It can be the most wonderful companion on our journey with Jesus as we look back and see how the prayers we prayed were answered. It can give us hope to keep trusting that we *are* being listened to and cared for and God *is* showing up for us along the path. It can even be a collection of letters to Him—a pouring out of our daily doubts and fears, the questions weighing on our hearts, and the unexpressed feelings we've been carrying.

Whatever it looks like, journaling can lighten our load and remind us that this journey we're on is headed somewhere good. We can be reminded that even when it seems like nothing is in our hands, it is all in the hands of Someone who knows exactly what He's doing with it. God delights in our drawing near to Him, heart to heart. His Word reminds us to never hold back: "Let us then with confidence draw near to the throne of grace, that we may receive mercy and find grace to help in time of need" (Hebrews 4:16 ESV). Some people find that they feel a special connection when they express themselves to Him through their written words. It's something to consider, remembering always that no matter how we choose to draw near, He will meet us where we are.

***Lord, may my words reveal my heart for You,***
***and may I always desire to draw near.***

# MAKE A DATE

*"I am the vine; you are the branches.*
*Whoever abides in me and I in him,*
*he it is that bears much fruit,*
*for apart from me you can do nothing."*

*JOHN 15:5 ESV*

You probably know what it's like to have a calendar brimming with commitments. Whether or not that's a season you're in right now, you know that those full-calendar days require a lot of prioritizing. If there's something that's important to you and you don't find a slot for it, it's just not happening. Here's a thought: Do you ever add a date with Jesus into those squares? Maybe you already have a daily time of prayer, or you may just talk with Him all day long. Especially in difficult times, that connection is an anchor for our souls. There's something extra special about making a date once in a while, though—just like you would meet a best friend for coffee, or go to a concert with your spouse, or take a child out for ice cream. Designating a place and setting aside some time means that person is important to you. You are looking forward to some one-on-one time with them. You may learn more about each other or share a new experience or find joy in something together. These are all things that can happen with Jesus. By setting aside time to be with Him, we are letting Him know we want to know Him more. And this can happen in so many places! A restaurant or coffee shop, a bike path or mountain trail, a gymnasium or auditorium. Wherever we are and whatever we're doing, being aware of His presence makes those moments sacred. After some time spent specifically with Him, we can have a new sense of how personal His love is for us. That's something we all need as we walk through times of grief.

We may not be making many dates at the moment, but the one connection that matters most is worth a mention on the calendar. And the beautiful thing about this date is that we can come as we are. We don't have to clean up; we don't have to be all smiles; we don't have to worry about being too chatty or not talkative enough. We can just rest in His presence and ask what He might have to speak to our hearts. No matter how we do it, this is something to consider as we lay out our days.

*Lord, thank You for Your loving presence.*
*Help me to always make time for You.*

# OUR FATHER

***This, then, is how you should pray:***
***"Our Father in heaven, hallowed be Your name,***
***Your kingdom come, Your will be done,***
***on earth as it is in heaven.***
***Give us today our daily bread.***
***And forgive us our debts, as we also have forgiven***
***our debtors. And lead us not into temptation,***
***but deliver us from the evil one."***

*MATTHEW 6:9–13 NIV*

Some days, we just don't know how to pray. Our hearts don't have the words, or we don't have the peace we need in our minds. We know we need that life-giving connection with God, but it's just not happening for us right now. Jesus gave His disciples a beautiful prayer that can help us on days like this. We may have prayed it many times before, but when we stop and reflect on the meaning of His words, we can find peace and encouragement.

"*Our Father in heaven*"—Abba or Daddy, our loving protector, provider, and guide who is above all, yet right here with us in every way—"*hallowed be your name*"—the name above every name, the holiest and purest we could ever imagine —"*your kingdom come, your will be done*"—Your way, Your plan, Your purpose—"*on earth as it is in heaven*"—here among us in this world, just as it is in the most loving, perfect place. "*Give us today our daily bread*"—we trust You to provide what we need each day, so we don't have to worry about tomorrow. "*And forgive us our debts, as we also have forgiven our debtors*"—have mercy on us for any wrongs we have done, just as we show mercy to others. "*And lead us not into temptation, but deliver us from the evil one*"—protect us from anything or anyone that would cause us to turn away from You. Keep us free from the enemy of our souls.

May these words comfort and encourage your heart anytime you are looking for a connection with your Father. He surely desires to deepen our understanding of Him in every way.

***Lord, thank You for providing***
***a beautiful prayer to help us connect with You.***
***May I be reminded of it often.***

# A TIME TO RENOVATE

*For we are co-workers in God's service;*
*you are God's field, God's building.*
I CORINTHIANS 3:9 NIV

If you've ever experienced construction in your home, then you know how unpredictable it can be. You may have begun with a cost estimate and a projected "finish" date, but you likely had to adjust your expectations along the way. No one wants to pay more or wait longer, but sometimes, in order to get the very best finished product, it's just necessary. When we experience the darker times in our lives, this is something unexpected that can happen to us. Our Creator, who sees the big picture for each of us, can use these times to make adjustments within us—just like those renovations. These aren't likely adjustments that *we* see as necessary for our faith to grow, but He knows just where we're headed, how we're getting there, and exactly what we need.

Hard times make us moldable—we're vulnerable, and we recognize that we're not in control. We can be open for Him to work in our lives, even if it's painful and uncomfortable at the moment. And just like someone having their home fixed up, it can cost more and last longer than we would hope. We must hold on to the truth that He is creating something beautiful in us, and it won't always feel like this. We can also remember that no matter how confusing or chaotic things may feel, we have the firm foundation of Jesus, and nothing can ever destroy that in our lives. Despite any worry, doubt, or fear, we stand on the solid ground that will last into eternity.

On days when it seems to be too much, when the journey feels overwhelming, consider drawing near to God in prayer. Ask Him to help you see the ways He's working in you, and trust that He has used this time in your life for great purpose. One day, you will see how carefully He created the blueprint of you.

***Lord, help me to be open to all the ways You are working in me during this time.***

# THE FAMILIAR THINGS

*"Comfort, comfort my people," says your God.*

*ISAIAH 40:1 ESV*

From the beginning of time, God has blessed human beings with the comfort of familiarity. He created us for connection, knowing that the faces and voices and gestures of our loved ones would become familiar and dear to us. He gave us the seasons of the year, knowing we would look forward to familiar signs of change as one season transitioned into another. He introduced us to tradition, a familiar way of celebrating and honoring special days in our lives. These things all help us to feel grounded. We are able to see patterns; we can sense the rhythms of life, and they give us comfort and assurance when things feel chaotic or uncertain.

In a time of loss, familiarity can be a blessing. We may be so used to it that we don't think about what it does for us, but it can be a healing thing to consider. Think of the loved ones around you. Who assures you with their familiar presence in your life? In what ways can you count on them to show up for you? This is part of God's plan to provide for you. And how about nature? What do you notice daily when you look out your window? Think of the way He designed every detail of creation, planning for certain beauties to return every season, knowing you'd find comfort in them. Now, think about the traditions you keep. What experiences can you count on each year? God has provided special days to look forward to and inspired you to set them aside in your own unique ways.

In these times of transition, when we may feel like we're adrift on a sea of uncertainty, reflecting on what is familiar gives us a sense of peace and assurance. We can be reminded that this is one way God has designed us to make our way through hard times. Keep holding on to those gifts He has given you, knowing that in that familiarity, He is making His presence known.

***Lord, thank You for providing what is familiar in my life. Help me to be aware of those blessings every day.***

# TALKING TO YOU

*And now, dear brothers and sisters, one final thing. Fix your thoughts on what is true, and honorable, and right, and pure, and lovely, and admirable. Think about things that are excellent and worthy of praise.*

*PHILIPPIANS 4:8 NLT*

It's been said that the human brain processes anywhere from sixty to seventy thousand thoughts per day. That's a lot of thinking! Add to that the fact that many of our thoughts are us talking to ourselves, and you realize how much influence you have—both as a talker and a listener. It's hard enough to keep those thoughts positive on good days; there's plenty of negativity in the world, and it can easily find its way into our heads and our hearts. But during our toughest days, it can be a true battle. We have an enemy that's all too eager to fill our minds with discouragement and despair.

Here's something that can easily be forgotten: *we can stand up for ourselves by speaking good things to ourselves*. We can remind ourselves that this is one of the hardest times in our lives, and we need plenty of grace and compassion each day to make it through. We can imagine what our loving Father would be saying to us, and we can repeat those words until they are rooted in our hearts. From the moment we wake up, we can speak words of encouragement to ourselves and try to become more and more aware throughout the day what path our thoughts are taking. Affirmations from God's Word are a wonderful way to keep those thoughts true and uplifting. Here are a few you may like to have on hand:

- *I am loved with an everlasting love* (Jeremiah 31:3 NIV).
- *I am strong, courageous, and not afraid, because the Lord my God is with me* (Deuteronomy 31:6 NIV).
- *I have patience and peace because God's timing is perfect* (Ecclesiastes 3:11 NIV).
- *I know that God's plans for me are good and filled with hope* (Jeremiah 29:11 NIV).
- *Jesus is my light that shines in the darkness, and the darkness cannot overcome it* (John 1:5 NIV).

May your mind be blessed with daily peace and assurance as you trust in Him.

***Lord, help me to speak good words to myself and to remember to give myself the compassion and grace that You show me every day.***

# BROKEN IN

*"Don't be afraid, for I am with you.*
*Don't be discouraged, for I am your God.*
*I will strengthen you and help you.*
*I will hold you up with My victorious right hand."*
*ISAIAH 41:10 NLT*

We all need new shoes once in a while. And it's possible, when we pull them on for the first time, that they may feel a little stiff and uncomfortable. It might take us some time walking around in them to break them in. At some point, though, they mold to our feet and give and bend just where we need them to. Life can feel like that sometimes. When we go through a transition, it changes us. We may have been comfortable and familiar with our old ways, but something unfamiliar comes along and it just doesn't feel right. Losing a loved one is like that—it brings us into a new place.

Times of grief can bring lots of change. They can uncover things we struggle with that we thought we had under control. They can lead us to realize our total dependence on God to see us through a day. They can give us new perspectives, make us realize things we take for granted, or teach us things about ourselves we never saw before. At some point, we may find that we've been inspired to do life differently, to incorporate into our lives the things we learned in the valley of loss. We may cherish the people around us more, be more thankful for the little things, or become more aware that we aren't promised tomorrow. In other words, there's a lot happening on this journey, and it can take a while to sense that comfortable, "broken in" feeling that finally comes as we live through change. Let us remind ourselves that this is a significant transition. We need plenty of time and space for readjustment and renewal. And the beautiful thing to remember is that God invites us to bring it all to Him. He will help us move forward as the best versions of ourselves; He just asks us to trust Him to lead us. What a gift to know that every part of our lives is in His hands.

*Lord, change is hard,*
*but I know You're always with me.*
*Help me to trust Your timing and*
*to know my life is in Your hands.*

GOD IS
OUR REFUGE
AND STRENGTH,
ALWAYS READY
TO HELP IN TIMES
OF TROUBLE.

PSALM 46:1 NLT

# HIS STRENGTH

*But He said to me, "My grace is sufficient for you, for My power is made perfect in weakness."*
*II CORINTHIANS 12:9 NIV*

Sometimes well-meaning people who know what we're going through will say things like, "The tough times make you stronger." But at the moment, it sure doesn't feel like that. The world celebrates strength—lifting up those with a tough exterior who seem to be blazing a trail of triumph in their lives. But we, as followers of Jesus, know there's a different kind of strength being formed in us, and it doesn't start with human confidence or self-motivation; it starts with vulnerability. In times of grief, we're led to surrender everything—our feelings, our expectations. . .even our relationships. There's so much stirring inside us, and we aren't the ones doing the stirring! As we seek to follow God through it all, we realize we are completely at His mercy. The truth is, we are always at His mercy, but some seasons reveal that truth more than others. We are vulnerable, and vulnerability can feel like weakness, and nobody wants to be weak. We can't imagine that any kind of strength could come out of this. How could

God possibly be working for our good? That's when we can remind ourselves of those who have gone before us, and all the places in His Word where He enters their situations of total helplessness and transforms them; He makes the impossible possible.

Our Father has a heart for the powerless. He will not leave us in our need. But as Isaiah 40:29–31 reminds us, one thing is required on our part, and that is *hope*: "He gives strength to the weary and increases the power of the weak. Even youths grow tired and weary, and young men stumble and fall; but those who hope in the Lord will renew their strength. They will soar on wings like eagles; they will run and not grow weary, they will walk and not be faint" (NIV). This strength is being created in you now, but it won't show up until later. That's where the hope comes in; we're called to hold on to it right now, no matter what. We will one day look back and marvel at all we made it through, and we will move forward with a new capacity to face life's most difficult days. Remember, what's happening within you is much deeper than feeling, and every day God is bringing you a little further along.

***Lord, You are my strength! Help me to hold on with hope, no matter what.***

# ALWAYS THERE

***God said, "My presence will go with you. I'll see the journey to the end."***
***EXODUS 33:14 THE MESSAGE***

Throughout our journeys on this earth, we learn that there will be some moments when we sense God's nearness and other moments when He feels far away. There are so many things that contribute to the ebb and flow of our spiritual lives. For some people, times of loss can be intimate times with Jesus. All the worldly distractions, along with the hustle and bustle of life, fall away, and we find ourselves heart to heart with Him, just praying to get through another day. For others, grief can make God seem distant. We don't have the warm, fuzzy feeling that we may have in times of joy. Our hearts are raw, and we can struggle with bitterness or anger toward Him. We may doubt His goodness or even His existence as we feel our way through what can be very dark times. But no matter how close or far away we feel, we can hang on to this one beautiful truth: *He has never moved*. Before we ever knew His Name—back when He had just spoken us into existence—He was with us. And since then, He has pursued us all our lives, showing up in so many ways, whether we realized it or not.

Reminding ourselves of those times when we have been aware of His presence can help us through times when we just aren't feeling it. We can recall moments when we were afraid, or doubtful, or lonely, and He came through with comfort and peace. Or what about times of praise and celebration? He may have filled our hearts to overflowing with hope and joy.

If there haven't been many times in your life that you can recall feeling His presence, consider asking Him to help you sense Him near today. Remember: our feelings can be all over the place, but God does not change. He is as near to you as He was in the very beginning. Just think. . .He had the *idea* of you, and ever since, He has looked for ways to draw you close. No matter how you feel right now, be encouraged in knowing He has never left your side.

***Lord, help me to be aware of Your presence beyond my feelings. Thank You for always being there.***

# COMFORT AND COMPANIONSHIP

*Two are better than one.*

*ECCLESIASTES 4:9 NIV*

There is no doubt that having to say goodbye to someone we love leaves an irreplaceable space in our lives—one we can't imagine filling with anyone or anything else. This is God's design, as He knit each of us together in a way that no other person could emulate. He gave us one-of-a-kind relationships, created to bring out certain things in us, to help mold us into the people He is calling us to be. What a gift every life is! As the psalmist reminded us, He has created our "inmost being" (Psalm 139:13 NIV) and we are "fearfully and wonderfully made" (Psalm 139:14 NIV). How blessed we are to be connected on this Earth with those people God gives to us, who are each unique expressions of His love.

As we move through this season, acknowledging the new and empty space that has been left, there is something comforting we can do. We can ask God to remind us how precious the people who surround us are. We can remember the relationships that we have today and strengthen our connections with those He has brought into our lives. We can even recognize His presence as we gather with others: "For where two or three gather in My name, there am I with them" (Matthew 18:20 NIV). Our loving Father never leaves us alone in our grief. If you find yourself feeling a sense of loneliness, consider coming to Him in prayer for companionship. There may be people in your life right now who He's calling to draw closer to you. He knows exactly what each relationship can bring to your heart. Jesus, who knows every hurt we could possibly experience, knew what it was like to lose someone precious to Him. He also knew the comfort of companions on the journey. After He learned that His cousin John the Baptist had died, He withdrew in a boat to be alone. Not long after, His disciples came to Him—a moment that surely comforted His heart. Each of His disciples were precious to Him in their own way, just like the people in our lives today, which is a beautiful thing to remember when that space in your life feels lonely. God has provided comfort and companionship for His beloved—*you*.

***Lord, remind me of the preciousness of the people in my life today. Help me find comfort in the companionship You provide.***

# HONEST WORDS

***Out of the depths I cry to you, Lord;***
***Lord, hear my voice.***
*PSALM 130:1–2 NIV*

What a gift we have in the Psalms—the people of God navigating their journeys, sometimes over the moon with joy and shouts of praise; other times, crawling along in tears, crying out, "Why, Lord?" or "How long?" As we read through these very human writings, it isn't hard to find ourselves there. Journeys of grief have a way of stripping away fluffy words and spiritual-sounding niceties. We come to God in our realest, rawest forms, speaking from broken hearts and crushed spirits, laying ourselves out before Him in the only way we know how. And in those humble, desperate places, He meets with us and cherishes our presence. He doesn't need the pomp and circumstance of super-spirituality to catch His attention; He simply longs to connect with us, heart to heart.

Would you ever consider writing your own psalm? Next time you're feeling the weight of this journey, try using a piece of paper and a pen to write a note to your loving Father. Let your words pour out without worrying about how they sound. Trust that He sees your heart and knows your struggle intimately. Feel the relief that comes from telling the truth about how you feel, and sense the connection God provides for a heart that seeks Him earnestly and honestly.

Keep your psalm and revisit it from time to time. Let it remind you of how God saw you through this time in your life. You are just as precious to Him as those who cried out thousands of years ago. And as His Word reminds us, "Weeping may stay for the night, but rejoicing comes in the morning" (Psalm 30:5 NIV). Remember, there will be times of praise in your future too. Hold on to that hope every step of the way.

***Lord, I bring You my heart today.***
***Please give me words for how I'm feeling,***
***and remind me that You hear them all.***

# LIFTED UP

***Let every living,***
***breathing creature praise God!***
***PSALM 150:6 THE MESSAGE***

During the most difficult times in our lives, our hearts carry a heaviness that's hard to shake. For many of us, it's a weight we wake up with and carry all the way till bedtime—a constant companion we'd rather do life without. Good things happen, we have moments of hope and happiness. . .but we are often drawn back to that burden, weighed down again by our loss. These are the seasons when it can be tough to imagine praising God. We may be clinging to Him, trusting Him to see us through, believing that He gives all things purpose, but *praise*? Who feels like holding their arms up with a "hallelujah" in times like this? And yet, God's Word reminds us how vital it is to praise Him, no matter what we're going through. It's more than a simple exercise in expressing joy—it's a deep, from-the-heart connection with the One who carries us. It isn't like He needs more praise from us; rather, He knows *we* need it. Those times when we find ourselves walking through darkness and discouragement are the times when we need it most.

If your heart is heavy today, take a moment to consider one thing you are grateful for, and thank God for it. Even if it's the tiniest thing, it's not small in His eyes. He who sees your hurt also sees your effort to praise Him in that moment. Know that He showers you with love in return. It may be something you do once a day, or it could become a wonderful habit. Regardless, it can bring a sense of lightness that your heart needs, and although these journeys are never easy, it is one way He brings hope and healing along the path.

***Lord, how can I be grateful today?  
Help me to lift my heart in praise to You.***

# TELLING THE TRUTH

***Look, the winter is past and the rains are over and gone. The flowers are springing up, the season of singing birds has come, and the cooing of turtledoves fills the air. The fig trees are forming young fruit, and the fragrant grapevines are blossoming.***

***SONG OF SOLOMON 2:11–13 NLT***

Redemption is a pattern we see throughout Scripture. Our Creator has a way of bringing light from darkness, beauty from ashes, hope from despair. It's hard to see sometimes, though, when we are recovering from loss. Our thoughts and feelings are strong. They can convince us that we're not getting anywhere, that God is not working to help us through, that things are going from bad to worse. Remember, in these times, *you don't have to believe what you think and feel.* You can acknowledge what's coming through your mind without letting it settle. It's like having birds flying around you but not allowing them to nest in your head. Your heart knows the truth, even when your brain is doubtful.

Here's what's true: you have a loving Father who is orchestrating each day to bring about your healing and to redeem this time in your life. You *are* moving forward, even when you don't feel it. And most importantly, God is going before you, preparing the way. You will not step into one day that He hasn't already laid out: "The Lord Himself goes before you and will be with you; He will never leave you nor forsake you. Do not be afraid; do not be discouraged" (Deuteronomy 31:8 NIV). Sometimes, on the hard days, it's good to preach this truth to yourself. Say it out loud if you need to: *The Lord goes before me. He will never leave me or forsake me. I will not be afraid or discouraged.* The more room His truth takes up in your mind, the less room there will be for doubt and discouragement. May each day bring loving reminders that this is a process, and that He is leading you through, step by step.

***Lord, You are my Redeemer. Help me to see the ways You are leading me through each day.***

# REMEMBERING LOVE

*We know how much God loves us,*
*and we have put our trust in His love.*
*I JOHN 4:16 NLT*

Some days, we may feel like there's just not enough within us to make it through. We may be feeling extra emotional, or unprepared in some way, or anxious, or fearful, or a whole host of other things. Seasons of grief can take away our sure footing and make us feel like we're constantly on shifting sand. In times like this, the absolute, most important thing we can hold on to is this truth: *God loves me.*

Remembering His love for us is everything. It can change the way we look at and experience even the toughest days. Instead of feeling like we have nothing to hold on to or nothing to offer, we are reminded that, in His love, we have everything. Because He loves us, we can trust His heart. That means that we will encounter nothing today that hasn't been lovingly allowed by Him and that He is using every tiny detail for our good. Because He loves us, we can trust that our lives are headed somewhere beautiful, and even our darkest times are woven into the masterpiece He is creating. Because He loves us, we have Jesus—Someone who has walked among us, cried our tears, and felt our deepest pain and understands all our thoughts, feelings, words, and actions. Because He loves us, we will never be alone. He is the one who inspires others to reach out with comfort and care, and in those times when we don't have human company, He offers us Himself to lean on, always willing to fill us with His peace.

Don't ever doubt His love for you. The more aware of His love you are, the more you can rest in Him and let life happen, knowing it's all in His hands. Remember, He cherishes you as a precious child: "See what kind of love the Father has given to us, that we should be called children of God; and so we are" (I John 3:1 ESV). You will never face a day without this love. It is all you will ever need.

***Lord, thank you for Your unfailing love.***
***I open my heart to You.***

# OUR PATH

***But the Lord's plans stand firm forever;***
***His intentions can never be shaken.***

*PSALM 33:11 NLT*

Sometimes we look at the hard seasons in our lives like detours—like things were going along well, and then we were faced with a loss, and suddenly life veered off the path we had hoped to stay on. But the truth is, this path has been part of our journey ever since we took our first breath. God knew when He created us exactly what we would walk through in this broken world. No experience is a surprise to Him. And because of His deep compassion for us and His understanding of our human struggles, He works in our lives to prepare us for the things that we will go through. This may not seem obvious to us when we're in the depths of our toughest days, but if we look back, we may see evidence of His plan—certain experiences or relationships or revelations He's provided that gave us something we'd need down the road, like faith, strength, courage, or hope. And not only has He prepared us for this time, but He has always known how He would carry us through it—healing our hearts, inspiring others to reach out to us with comfort and support, helping us to make it one more day when we feel like giving up. We may see Him as Someone who has shown up to help in our time of need, but the truth is, He's always been there, orchestrating our good times and our hard times with eternal wisdom and loving care. And finally, He knows just how He will use this time in our future, shaping us into who we're becoming. He already knows all the ways He is preparing us for other things we'll experience in life, and who He might call us to reach out to when others face the same struggles. He has woven our lives together in such a way that everything is somehow connected. Let us remember this when it feels like life has taken a wrong turn. Our Creator doesn't make detours. He just gives us what we need to finish the course.

***Lord, help me to remember that You have always had great plans for me. Thank You for all the ways You have guided my life.***

# HAPPY PLACES

***So whether you eat or drink or whatever you do, do it all for the glory of God.***

*I CORINTHIANS 10:31 NLT*

Sometimes, during our most difficult seasons, we stop doing some of the things that usually bring us joy. Whether it's gardening, baking, reading, participating in sports, watching a new TV series, doing a creative hobby, spending time with friends, volunteering. . .the list goes on. God has given each of us those bright spots in our lives, and we know we can turn to them anytime we need a little boost. But what happens when we stop feeling motivated to go to our happy places? It may be hard enough just to face the day right now, let alone make plans to do something that lifts our spirits.

First, we need to realize that those things *will* make us smile once again. It may not be today or tomorrow, but we *will* make it through the heaviness and have lighter spirits and a brighter outlook. Second, let us remember that sometimes, if we take an action, our feelings will follow. If it has been a while since we've done something that brings us joy, we can always give it a try. Yes, it may not feel just like we're used to. We may wish for that familiar experience, but we can remind ourselves that we're in a time of transition. We can give those things a try with gratitude for any bit of lightness and goodness they may bring. And lastly, we can consider doing something new. Is there anything you've always wanted to try? Who do you know who has taken opportunities that have inspired you? Have you been invited to join anyone in an activity? Yes, these things may sound intimidating or exhausting right now, and that's okay. But there may be a time when you're ready to take a few more steps in your healing journey, and you may wish to give those things a try. Ask your heavenly Father to help you sense His presence with you no matter what you do, and you can be sure that He will cover it all with His love. Whatever He intends for you to experience will be yours.

***Lord, thank You for the bright spots You bless me with. When the time is right, help me to choose those things that make me smile again.***

# BRIGHTER DAYS

***"So also you have sorrow now,***
***but I will see you again, and your hearts will rejoice,***
***and no one will take your joy from you."***
*JOHN 16:22 ESV*

People who have walked this journey of grief will often say that loss is something we never truly get over. It is true that we will grieve to the depth that we have loved, and that the love we shared will always be a part of us. The person we have lost will come to mind for the rest of our lives, and we will miss them greatly. But as our hearts heal and God does His good work within us, our remembrance will be transformed into something beautiful. Today, this may be impossible to imagine. Those raw feelings of hurt and sadness can be overwhelming, and we can find ourselves wondering how things will ever change. All we can do in these times is hold on to hope and trust that our loving Father will lead us through, one day at a time.

It can help to look forward to the things we may experience when some time has passed on this path of healing. One of those things is gratitude: God brings joy out of our gratitude. As we continue to look to

Him to guide us, He can bless us with a deep sense of gratitude for the life of our loved one, no matter how many years they were given on Earth. When they come to mind, so will the blessings we knew because of them. Another thing is appreciation: losing someone dear to us often reminds us not to take anyone for granted. The people God has placed in our lives are there for specific reasons; He has a purpose for every connection. Our remembrance of our loved one can inspire us to treasure those around us, to take advantage of every opportunity to be present with them. And finally, we can be reminded of our purpose. We know what it is like to say goodbye to someone dear to us, and we can help others down the road who are going through the same thing. We can ask God to direct us to those in need and be blessed to reach out. Remember, it's a journey, but healing is always happening.

***Lord, help me to hold on to You and trust You for brighter days ahead.***

NOW MAY
THE LORD
OF PEACE HIMSELF
GIVE YOU PEACE
AT ALL TIMES AND
IN EVERY WAY.

II THESSALONIANS 3:16 NIV

*Dear Friend,*

This book was prayerfully crafted with you, the reader, in mind. Every word, every sentence, every page was thoughtfully written, designed, and packaged to encourage you—right where you are this very moment. At DaySpring, our vision is to see every person experience the life-changing message of God's love. So, as we worked through rough drafts, design changes, edits, and details, we prayed for you to deeply experience His unfailing love, indescribable peace, and pure joy. It is our sincere hope that through these Truth-filled pages your heart will be blessed, knowing that God cares about you—your desires and disappointments, your challenges and dreams.

*He knows. He cares. He loves you unconditionally.*

**BLESSINGS!**
**THE DAYSPRING BOOK TEAM**

---